Active PARENTING Now in 3™

by Michael H. Popkin, Ph.D.

To my parents, Naomi and Harry Popkin
To the memory of my mother, Mona Rubin Popkin
To my wife and parenting partner, Melody Popkin
And to our children, Megan and Benjamin Popkin

Thank you for the gift of family.

ISBN 1-59723-080-4

Photography by Sonny Senser of Santaguida Photography and Michael H. Popkin
Cover design by Gabrielle Jenkins
Interior design by Rachel Metzger

Acknowledgements

Active Parenting Now in 3 is based on the time-tested theories of some of the great psychologists of the twentieth century. Chief among them are two Austrian psychiatrists who, though now deceased, continue to exert a profound influence on how we can effectively parent our children. Their names are Alfred Adler and Rudolf Dreikurs. I respectfully acknowledge that their contributions lie at the heart of this program.

Complementing the theories of Adler and Driekurs, I have included communication skills that have grown out of the pioneering work of Carl Rogers, Robert Carkhuff, and Thomas Gordon. I am also indebted to the work of Haim Ginott, Albert Ellis, and Milton Erickson.

I also acknowledge and thank my two mentors, Professor Kenneth Matheny of Georgia State University and Professor Oscar Christensen of the University of Arizona. You are much more a part of this program than the one story that I "borrowed" from each of you. Thanks are also expressed to Professor Roy Kern of Georgia State University, who first introduced me to parenting education some 30 years ago, and to Frank Walton, who just keeps on encouraging.

Finally, I would like to acknowledge the tremendous work of the staff at Active Parenting Publishers, who continue to make the dream of Active Parenting a daily reality. A special thank you to Rachel Metzger, Director of Product Development, and her team, Carol Keller and Gabrielle Jenkins, who saw this project through to completion. And to a very special employee of the company, my father, Harry G. Popkin—social worker, camp director, role model, and inspiration. It's been great working with you, Dad.

Michael H. Popkin
Atlanta, Georgia

Table of Contents

Table of Contents (continued)

Table of Contents (continued)

Preface

Active Parenting Publishers, founded in 1980, created the world's first video-based parenting education program. The need for such an innovation in parenting education was based on two beliefs about parenting in our modern democratic society:

1. Parenting well is extremely important.

2. Parenting well is extremely difficult.

It is also assumed that most parents want to parent well, but have not been given the necessary skills or support.

This lack of training can be disastrous in our modern society, where children openly reject traditional parenting methods. Everywhere, we find parents and children engaging in frustrating struggles for power. Families often become an energy drain and source of frustration rather than a support network and source of satisfaction. Worse, many children are not developing the basic qualities of character necessary for thriving in our modern society: courage, responsibility, cooperation, respect and self-esteem.

Consequently, many parents of young children express fear about the choices their children will make when they become teenagers. This fear may be well founded. Teenage drug use, pregnancy, abortion, crime, AIDS, and suicide all remain at frighteningly high levels.

Obviously, parenting is not the only influence on a child's development, but it is the one we can do the most about. This Parent's Guide has been designed to teach you a method of parenting and problem solving that will help you prepare your children to courageously meet the challenges life will pose. And it will help you build relationships that bring joy and satisfaction for a lifetime.

At the end of our lives, we will not remember how much money we made, how many ball games we watched, or how many things we possessed. What will come back to us in a brilliant and blinding light is the quality of the relationships we formed with those we loved: our friends, our spouses, our children.

Communication and Cooperation

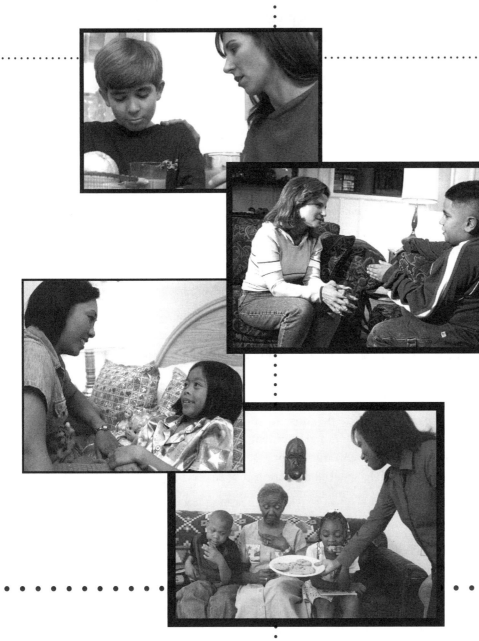

Perhaps the truest thing that can be said about parenting is that it requires a lot of energy. It is a tremendously "active" undertaking, requiring a 24/7 commitment with a myriad of skills ranging from discipline to communication and support. Children, it seems, respond better to actions than to words. And so, to be an effective parent is to be an active parent. This is one of the reasons we have chosen the name *Active Parenting Now* for this guide.

We also think of the word "active" as a contrast to the "reactive" approach used by most parents. Reactive parents wait until their children push them to their limits, then they react. Often they react with frustration, anger, and random discipline ... or as one mother put it, "the screech and hit" school of parenting. When parents "react" rather than "act," they are allowing the child to control both the situation and the parent's own emotions. Problems tend to continue or even get worse as parent and child re-act the same frustrating scenes over and over.

Our philosophy in Active Parenting Now is that it is the job of the parent, rather than the child, to play the leadership role in the family.

Part of the problem is that most parents do not have a consistent approach to parenting. They use a little of what their parents did, a little of the exact opposite of what their parents did, and a little of what they picked up from friends, books, and magazine articles. Our philosophy in *Active Parenting Now* is that it is the job of the parent, rather than the child, to play the leadership role in the family. This guide will help you clarify your own goals for your child and teach you effective methods for leading your child toward them. But it will do more. It will also teach you a consistent model of parenting, enabling you to act with confidence and clarity as you encounter the many challenges parents face.

There are other reasons we chose to emphasize the word "active." This is an age of active people, who are engaged in a host of active pursuits: jobs and careers, community work, political causes, the arts, hobbies, and sports. The fact that you are reading this book shows that you are one of these active people; you are taking steps toward improving your family interactions, and you are seeking information to help you excel as a parent. So *Active Parenting Now* is for active people like you.

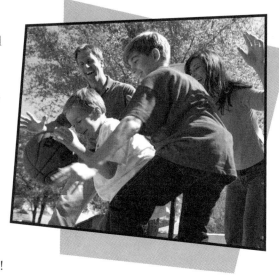

A word of caution: this model has been used effectively by millions of parents, counselors, teachers and psychologists. It works! However, it is put into use by human beings, and human beings, as we all know, are imperfect. We make mistakes. During this workshop you will probably become aware of two kinds of mistakes of your own:

First, you may realize or recall mistakes you have made in the past in your own parenting. Almost everyone does. It is important that you recognize these mistakes, but it is much more important that you let them go. They are in the past, and it is useless to dwell on them now. It's much more productive to concentrate on being a more effective parent in the present and in the future!

Second, you will make further mistakes as you learn these new skills. Mistakes are part of the learning process, and they happen to everyone using new skills. So it is important that you accept your mistakes without punishing yourself for being imperfect. If you are too hard on yourself, you not only make yourself feel bad, you also put limits on your learning. This is because when we feel criticized, even by ourselves, we become defensive.

Soon we don't even admit our mistakes to ourselves, and we lose the valuable opportunity to correct and improve our performance. Mistakes are for learning; please be gentle with yourself!

Parenting: The Most Important Job

If the future of our society is our children, then the key to that future rests primarily with parents and teachers.

Parenting, though still one of the most underrated jobs in our society, is beginning to attract some of the attention and consideration it deserves. After all, if the future of our society is our children, then the key to that future rests primarily with parents and teachers. Many schools, religious institutions, mental health centers, and other community organizations are responding to this reality by offering support to parents through programs such as *Active Parenting Now.*

The Purpose of Parenting

Success at any job first requires a sound understanding of its purpose. The basic purpose of parenting has not changed throughout history. We can state it like this:

> ***The purpose of parenting is to protect and prepare our children to survive and thrive in the kind of society in which they live.***

Although this purpose has not changed over the years, our society has changed in the following ways:

It is more dangerous. The illegal drugs available to today's children and teens are easier to find and more harmful than ever. Crimes against children — and crimes by children — are more numerous than when we were growing up. There is a serious problem with violence in schools and the risk of terrorism is something we are all concerned about. Even sexual activity can now be life threatening.

This poses a difficult problem for parents. Part of our purpose as parents is to protect our children so they will survive. Yet if we overprotect them, we are not preparing them to survive and thrive on their own. Keep in mind that the job of parenting is to work yourself out of a job! That means preparing your child for independence. Three things will help you do this:

1. **Talk with other adults to get an idea of what risks are reasonable for your child to take in your community.** For example, how old should they be to be left home alone and where is it safe for them to play?

2. **Join with other associations, parent support groups, or other organizations.** Work within your community to make it a better place to rear children.

3. **Allow your child to develop independence gradually.** *Active Parenting Now in 3* will help you learn the skills that will encourage your child to build independence. Because children develop through various stages, appropriate behavior at one age may not be appropriate at another. There are many good books available to help you know what to expect at these ages and stages of development. Talking with your child's teachers and other parents will help you, too.

Society is more diverse and more just. If the bad news about modern society is that it has become more dangerous, the good news is that it has also become more just. We can be proud that our country was founded on the principle that all people are created equal. In fact, this concept of equality is a hallmark of democratic societies throughout the world.

Unfortunately, the word "all" in the United States of America in 1776 really meant all white males who owned land. The rest were not even allowed to vote. But the ball of social progress was moving, and during the next 150 years such milestones as the end of slavery, the beginning of the Labor movement, and the right of women to vote showed that we intended to fulfill the promise of democracy. Then, in the 1950s with the advent of television, the movement for social equality took a giant leap forward. When

Today's children do not want to be "seen and not heard" or otherwise treated disrespectfully.

Martin Luther King, Jr. spoke of his dream of equality for all humankind, the ever-present eye of the cameras carried his message throughout the world. One group after another — African-Americans, Native Americans, Hispanics, Asians, students, women — began to demand that they, too, be treated as equals. Today, no group wants to be treated as inferior, to unquestioningly do what they are told, to speak only when spoken to, or to otherwise allow themselves to be treated disrespectfully.

The atmosphere of equality in which our children live has created a new challenge for today's active parents. We must now contend with a generation of children who are no longer comfortable with their traditional role of inferiority in society. Today's children do not want to be "seen and not heard" or otherwise treated disrespectfully.*

The parenting skills taught in this book take into account the need for new approaches to leadership in a society of equals. However, the concept that "all (people) are created equal" does not mean that all people are created the same. Differences between people range from the obvious, such as how we look, to the subtle, such as our dreams and values. People also have different roles they play and different responsibilities depending on those roles.

The parent's role is that of a leader, while the child more often plays the role of the learner.

In spite of these differences, we are each considered of equal value and worth under our Constitution. This means we are entitled to equal protection under the law, equal opportunity for employment, an equal right to make our opinions known, and an equal right to be treated respectfully, to name a few.

Likewise, in a family parents and children are equal in some ways and different in others. One big way that parents and children are still different is in the roles they play. The parent's role is that of a leader, while the child more

---

*Note: Because Active Parenting Now was first published in the United States, historical references refer to this democratic society. Because each democratic society has its own story to tell, parents in countries other than the U.S. may wish to share ways in which their own struggle for equality was achieved.

often plays the role of the learner. As the leaders in the family, parents have certain rights and responsibilities that differ from those of their children. For example, we have the responsibility of providing food, clothing, shelter, and protection for our children. We also have the right to drive, vote, use alcohol, and other privileges that are not available to children.

We have the authority to decide many of the matters that affect the lives of our children including matters of health, safety, and family values.

In addition, we have the authority to decide many of the matters that affect the lives of our children, including matters of health, safety, and family values. Since this includes how we decide to parent, we will look at the concept of authority more closely later in the chapter.

Society changes at an increasing rate. Today's high-tech society changes faster than any in history. Jobs, even industries, that thrive in one decade may be gone the next, replaced by new technologies that were undiscovered when we were in school. Success in such a high-change society requires children to do much more than just learn. They must also learn how to adapt to change and keep learning. Neither blind obedience nor an attitude of complacency is likely to provide them with the skills and character necessary to navigate the current of change that is likely to come. This guide will help you learn methods for empowering your children to be decision makers, problem solvers, team players, and lifelong learners—regardless of what career paths they may choose.

Changes in family make up. Change in society has also affected the very make-up of families. The traditional family of two biological parents and children is no longer the norm. More than half of all children will find themselves in single-parent families or families blended together with parents and children from previous marriages. Many other children will live with grandparents, homosexual parents, or other caregivers with whom they share no previous ties at all. No matter what type of family you are a part of, the skills in this book will help you develop the kind of relationship you and your child need to thrive now and later. Of course, there are other issues that we will not address that are specific to your situation, and we encourage you to check the resource section in the back of the book for more information that can help.

The Risks: Drugs, Sexuality, and Violence

The risks associated with drugs, sexuality, and violence are greatest during the teen years. However, what you do now as parents will make a huge difference in what your children will do later when you are not around. We will focus on three major ways to help you reduce the risk that your children will become harmfully involved in these three areas:

1. Build character and develop skills in your child.

Using the active parenting skills taught in this program will help build five important qualities of character— courage, self-esteem, responsibility, cooperation, and respect.

Using the active parenting skills taught in this guide will help build five important qualities of character—courage, self-esteem, responsibility, cooperation, and respect. This guide focuses on ways you can instill these characteristics, and many others, in your child. It also helps you develop the personal skills in your children that they will need to succeed—including problem solving, communication, anger management, and academic success. By developing these characteristics and personal skills we give our children a strong foundation from which to resist easy answers to life's problems, answers such as tobacco, alcohol and other drugs, reckless sexuality, and violence.

2. Build a strong relationship with your kids.

Our ability to influence the values our children will form and the decisions they will make is to a large extent dependent on the quality of our relationship with them. If our relationship is mostly negative, kids often reject even our good ideas. They are quick to rebel to show us that we can't push them around. Sometimes this rebellion takes the form of drugs, sexuality, and violence as they intentionally reject our values in these matters. The active model of parenting that we will be learning minimizes this risk while still empowering you to be the leader in the family. The methods taught throughout *Active Parenting Now in 3* are specifically aimed at building a strong parent-child relationship from which your influence can be effective.

3. Talk persuasively about the risks.

Once you have established a positive relationship with your child, it is important to talk about the specific risks involved with drugs, sexuality, and violence. You want to be as persuasive as possible in making your case and winning over their attitudes, because these are areas in which they will ultimately decide what to do. Discipline can be helpful, but discipline alone is not enough to win the battle for their minds. We will discuss effective communication skills in this chapter—skills that you are encouraged to use to talk with children about these and other important issues in their lives.

The more you can enrich your relationship with your child, the more he will allow you to be an influence in his life.

Your Child's Character

Because you will not always be there to ensure that your child makes good decisions, it is important that he develop an underlying framework of beliefs, attitudes, and values that will help him steer a successful course on his own. This is commonly referred to as "character," and it is one of the most important concepts in parenting. Although there are many qualities of character that you will want to instill in your children, we think there are five that are especially critical for success in today's high-tech, diverse, and democratic society:

A child's courage enables the child to try, fail, and try again, until she masters the challenges life presents.

Courage is the first. The psychologist Alfred Adler once said that if he could give one gift to a child, it would be courage. If a child is courageous, he reasoned, that child can learn everything else she needs to learn. Coupled with parental guidance, a child's courage enables the child to try, fail, and try again, until he masters the challenges life presents. With too little courage, the child gives up easily or does not try at all. Fear leads to failure, and failure reinforces fear. Such a cycle of discouragement supports a lifelong attitude of regret and resentment. Courage is a foundation upon which the child constructs his personality. It is at the heart of human potential. In this course we consider courage to be so essential to the child's development that we devote much of the third chapter to methods of encouraging children, and we will be referring to courage again and again.

Self-esteem is the second quality necessary for thriving in a democratic society. Simply stated, self-esteem is the opinion we have of ourselves. When a child's self-esteem is high, she sees herself as a capable human being who has a good opportunity to succeed at challenges. She also knows that even failure is nothing more than an opportunity for learning, so when she doesn't succeed at first, she does not give up. This perception of herself as a winner gives the child the courage to tackle life's problems through positive behavior, and to take advantage of the wonderful opportunities available in a democratic society. We will explore the critical connection between self-esteem, courage, and behavior in Chapter Three.

Democracy demands that its members make decisions and accept responsibility for the consequences of those decisions.

A sense of **responsibility** is the third quality a child needs to thrive. Democracy demands that its members make decisions and accept responsibility for the consequences of those decisions. Without individual responsibility, our cherished freedoms will give way to governmental responsibility, where the state will make decisions for us.

With freedom and choice comes the responsibility for the consequences of those choices. The reality of our society is that its children will be called upon to make thousands of choices, and they will be held responsible for their choices by experiencing the consequences that follow. Some of these choices will be life and death matters. They will be offered drugs; will they choose to accept? They will face choices about drinking, sex, crime, dropping out, and even suicide. And their parents won't always be there to tell them what to do. But if they have been prepared to make responsible decisions, and have developed the courage to stand behind these decisions, they will be prepared to meet these challenges. We will explore methods designed to teach responsibility to children throughout the program and especially in Chapter Two.

Cooperation from the child cannot be demanded; it must be won.

Cooperation is the fourth essential quality children need to develop in order to thrive. In some circles a great deal of emphasis has been placed on competition as the road to success. In reality it has always been those individuals who have been aware of the magic of teamwork who have moved society forward. Helping a child learn that life is neither dependent nor independent, but rather an interdependent experience, is a cornerstone of *Active Parenting Now in 3*. In a society of equals, cooperation skills have high value, and the child who can cooperate is far more likely to survive and thrive than one who has never learned how. Ideally, the relationship of child and parent is one of cooperation rather than conflict. But cooperation from the child cannot be demanded; it must be won. In each session we will focus on a particular method of achieving cooperative relationships between parent and child through Family Enrichment Activities. In addition, a large part of Chapter One is devoted to teaching ways of winning cooperation through effective communication skills.

Respect is the fifth quality that we will address, and we will do so in this opening chapter, because it is the cornerstone of life in a democratic society. Teaching our children to respect themselves and others begins at home, but it pays dividends in every area in which they will become involved. Respect is about appreciating the worthwhile qualities in ourselves and others and demonstrating this through actions as well as attitude.

Styles of Parenting

Our goal as parents, then, is to instill in our children the skills and character that will enable them to survive and thrive in our fast-changing, diverse, democratic society. This is our responsibility and we have the authority to get the job done. After all, even in a society of equals, authorities still exist. The president of a corporation, the police officer on the street, and the principal in the school are examples of people who have the authority to make final decisions in their domains—and the responsibility to enforce those decisions. They are the leaders. However, there's not much use being a leader if no one is willing to follow you. Here, then, is an important principle of leadership:

Leaders get their ultimate authority from those they lead.

The same is true for parents. We are the authorities in our families. But to be effective, we must have the cooperation of our children. Let's look at three types of leadership and how effective each is likely to be in our current society.

1. Autocratic Style: The Dictator

A **dictator** is one who has abso-
lute control, and the autocratic
parent is all-powerful in dictating
the lives of his or her children.
This parent is a dominating figure
who rewards and punishes to
enforce his orders. Children are
told what to do, how to do it,
and when to do it. There is little
or no room for them to question,
challenge or disagree. The dictator method of parenting worked
reasonably well in times when
inequality was normal between
people, but it works poorly in
today's time of equality.

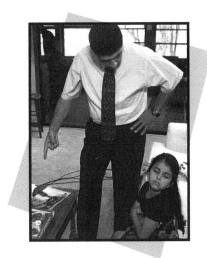

Children who grow up in autocratic families seldom thrive. They either
have their spirits broken and give up, or, more often, they rebel. This rebellion usually happens during the teen years, because the child has developed
enough power to fight back. The dictator has been the typical parenting
style for so many generations that teenage rebellion has come to be accepted
by many experts as "normal." This is a mistake. Teenagers do not have to
rebel to become independent.

The dictator can be described as using **"limits without
freedom."** This style can be depicted as a closed circle.

To his credit, the dictator does understand the need children have for limits.
He has the emotional strength and willingness to get involved and to stand
firm. But he often goes too far.

You are tending toward the autocratic style of parenting when you say things like:

> *"Because I'm the parent and I said so!"*
>
> *"As long as you live under my roof, you'll obey my rules."*
>
> *"When you are the parent, you can decide what to do."*

...and when you do things like:

- *tell your child what to wear.*
- *find yourself angry and yelling often.*
- *often ground or punish your child in other ways.*

2. Permissive Style: The Doormat

Permissive parents are often those who react strongly against the harsh and uncompromising autocratic method. Permissive parents allow their children to "do their own thing" too much of the time. In such households, there is little respect for order and routine, and few limits are placed on anyone's freedom. Many such parents behave like doormats, allowing their children to walk all over them. Some of these parents want to be firmer but do not know the words or discipline skills to use. One of the main drawbacks of this style is the feeling of insecurity which plagues children reared this way. They have almost no sense of belonging, and because they have not learned to cooperate, they are often difficult to live with.

Children with permissive parents are often pampered and accustomed to getting their own way. When someone outside the family finally tells them that rules apply to them also, these children or teens frequently rebel. It is difficult to get a child who is used to a lifestyle with no limits to voluntarily begin obeying rules.

The doormat approach can be described as **"freedom without limits,"** and can be shown as a squiggle line, representing freedom run rampant.

Although the permissive parent's desire to share power with their children and allow them freedom of choice is a good thing, they often go too far.

You are tending towards the permissive style of parenting when you say things like:

> *"I don't think that's a good idea…but, well…okay, if you really want to."*
> *"Do you really need this? Oh, all right. Here's the money."*
> *"I sure wish you'd help out around here."*

…and when you do things like:

- *allow her to go to bed whenever she feels like it.*
- *routinely do his homework with him or go to school to intervene for him often.*
- *give in to her unreasonable demands because you're afraid she will become angry or sad.*

3. Authoritative Style: The Active Parent

The **authoritative** style is, in some respects, the middle ground between the autocratic and permissive styles, but it is also much more. In an active household, freedom is an ideal, but so are the rights of others and the responsibilities of all. The parent is the leader who encourages cooperation and stimulates learning. There is order and routine, and every person is an important member of the family.

The active parent acknowledges our democratic heritage and the role of social equality among all human beings in two important ways:

1. Children are treated with dignity and respect, even when their parents discipline them.

2. Children are entitled to respectfully express their thoughts and feelings to their parents. In this way they are given the right to influence the decisions that affect their lives. This is consistent with life in a democratic society:

Democracy does not mean you will always get your way.
It means you will always get your say.

 The authoritative style can be called **"freedom within limits,"** and can be symbolized by a squiggly line within the limits of a circle.

In fact, it could be shown as "freedom within expanding limits." As the child assumes more and more responsibility, the parent gradually expands the limits, until eventually a young adult leaving home has the same amount of independence as you or I do.

You are tending toward the active style of parenting when you say things like:

"I know you're disappointed, but you can't go. Here's why..."
"Sure we can talk about it. What's your idea?"
"I know you can handle it. But if you need some help, just let me know."

...and when you do things like:

- *involve your child in deciding who will do which family chores.*
- *give her the full responsibility for her homework, monitoring her just a little.*
- *show an active interest in his education by discussing his subjects with him regularly and attending school functions.*
- *involve her in the discipline process by talking with her about your expectations and the consequences for breaking agreements.*
- *letting him know what you like about him and encouraging him often.*
- *talking with her about topics—such as drug use, sexuality, and violence—in a calm and non-judgmental manner.*

Two Keys to Active Parenting: Mutual Respect and Participation

Parenting successfully in a democratic society is like any other type of effective leadership in a democratic society. It requires *respect* for those who are being led and it requires their *participation* in the decision-making process. Without respect and participation a leader will eventually find herself with a rebellion on her hands. Let's see how these two key concepts can make you a more effective parent and leader in your family (or for that matter, manager at work!)

Mutual Respect

Our children are growing up in a society in which people are very sensitive to signs of disrespect. In fact, to disrespect somebody is often considered a personal affront, one that can even lead to violence.

Likewise, learning to respect oneself regardless of strengths, weaknesses, family, culture, or heritage is a building block for self-esteem and success. When we show our children respect, even when we are angry or providing discipline, we help them learn to respect themselves while demonstrating how to treat others respectfully.

Treating our children respectfully is also a good way to teach them how to treat us respectfully.

Treating our children respectfully is also a good way to teach them how to treat us respectfully. As the author, Bernard Malamud once wrote, "respect is what you have to have in order to get." In other words, if we want someone to treat us respectfully, even our children, then we have to be willing to treat them respectfully, too. This concept of "mutual respect," as Rudolf Dreikurs called it, is often easier said than done. Showing children respect means not yelling, cursing, calling them names, being sarcastic, or otherwise speaking to them in ways you would not want them speaking to you. There are also countless more subtle forms of disrespect to guard against. For example, an overprotective parent who is quick to jump in to solve a child's problem—without giving her a chance to struggle to find a solution for herself—is being disrespectful. A parent who always insists on doing what he wants and never compromising to do what the child wants is also showing disrespect.

When we catch ourselves treating our child disrespectfully, it is wise to smile, apologize, and if appropriate, make amends.

Examples:

> *"I'm sorry I yelled at you. That wasn't very respectful. Let me try again more calmly to tell you why I was angry."*
>
> *"I apologize for not calling to tell you I would be late. That wasn't respectful. How can I make it up to you?"*

Teaching our children to show respect to others begins with insisting on their showing us respect. This requires teaching on our part, as well as the use of the discipline skills we will be learning in Chapter Two. The parent who has been careful to show her child respect all along is on solid ground when it comes to correcting the child's disrespectful behavior.

Examples:

> *"I don't talk to you that way. Please do not talk to me that way."*
>
> *"I don't talk to you that way and I will not allow you to talk to me that way."*
>
> *"I want the two of you to stop right now. We don't talk to each other that way in our family."*

Teaching our children to show respect to others begins with insisting on their showing us respect.

As we will see in Chapter Two, when our words alone are not enough to correct misbehavior, we want to use a logically connected consequence to help get our message through.

Examples:

> *"Either talk to me without yelling or go to your room."*
>
> *"Either share the remote without fighting or there'll be no TV at all."*
>
> *"Either talk to me respectfully about not letting you watch a PG 13 movie or there will be no movies at all this week."*

Finally, the respect with which we treat our spouses, significant others, and even strangers sets an example for our children. When mutual respect is a cornerstone of your own interactions with people, as well as a strong family value, your children come to adopt it almost without trying.

Participation

A child will resist a parent who robs her of a chance to share in the decisions that affect her life.

The second key to active parenting, ***participation,*** involves one of the single most powerful forces in existence. This concept is so powerful that nations will go to war to preserve their right to choose how to live their lives. When we say that the hallmark of the active style of parenting is "freedom within limits," what we are really talking about is the freedom of the child to participate in decisions that affect his life.

Just as a people will rise up and overthrow a dictator, a child will resist a parent who robs her of this chance to participate. The parent who is neither a dictator nor a doormat, but an active leader in the family, will use this knowledge to handle problems and teach responsibility.

The Method of Choice.

The freedom to choose is tremendously empowering to children.

Choice is power. As the leader of your family, you can give your child choices that are appropriate for his age and level of responsibility. This, again, is the idea of freedom within expanding limits. The freedom to choose is tremendously empowering to children. And because you exercise your authority to limit what choices the child is allowed to make, family rules and values are not sacrificed.

Even young children can be given simple choices. Allowing your child the opportunity to practice decision making can become a regular part of your daily routine. This can also be useful in helping resolve conflicts. Consider this common situation: getting your child dressed. After unsuccessfully trying to coerce Austin into wearing his white shirt, Katy gives Austin a choice.

> *Katy: Would you rather wear this white shirt or the blue one?*
> *Austin: The blue one.*

This gives Austin some power over the decisions that affect his life, so he has less need to rebel. He chooses the blue one, which is acceptable to Katy.

Had he chosen a shirt that was unacceptable for the situation, Katy would have limited his choice.

Katy: I'm sorry, Austin, the T-shirt with spaghetti stains just isn't appropriate for going out. Let's stick with these two...this white one, or this blue one.

As children get older, the choices they are given can become more open-ended. So instead of either the blue or white shirt, you might simply ask the child what he would like to wear. The following are some examples of choices you can use.

Ages 4-7	Ages 8-12
"Would you like orange juice or grapefruit juice this morning?"	"Would you like to help me do the grocery shopping and help choose what we buy?"
"Can you put this away yourself, or would you like some help?"	"Do you prefer to set homework time for before dinner or afterwards?"
"Would you like to pick out a book or would you like me to choose a book for your bedtime story?"	"Would you rather go visit Grandma on Saturday or Sunday?"
"Would you like to take your bath now or after one more song?"	"Which chores would you like to do?"

A word of caution: Don't get carried away and make everything a choice. One parent gave her daughter so many choices that she had to choose from over a dozen different toothbrushes just to brush her teeth at night! No wonder it took forever to get to bed. Sometimes children want and need a firm but friendly decision from a parent. At other times, a limited set of choices is appreciated.

The Beauty of Problems

Those who succeed in our society are able to handle problems effectively.

One of the realities of life—whether at home, at work, or in the community—is that problems will arise. This is true for successful people and groups just as it is true for those who are unsuccessful. The difference is that those who succeed in our society are able to handle problems effectively. People who get bogged down in self-pity, play the blame game, make excuses, or make the same mistakes over and over again usually live with fear and anxiety. However, successful people seem to have the *courage* to cope with problems head on, the *self-esteem* to believe they will find a solution, the *responsibility* to accept ownership of the problem, the *cooperation* and *mutual respect* to work with others in handling the problem, and the *skills* necessary to find effective solutions.

Where did they learn all of this? Most likely from dealing with other problems, as children and then as adults, inside the family and out. Problems are a great resource for teaching our children much of what we want them to know. So, when a problem does occur, the active parent will take a deep breath and recognize that, in spite of the inconvenience involved, a wonderful teaching opportunity has just emerged.

To help you take advantage of these opportunities, much of this book is organized around the concept of handling problems. We will begin by looking at ways to build a cooperative relationship with your children. Then we will look at ways you can help them learn how to work with you to solve the problems they own responsibility for handling. In later chapters we will include discipline skills that can help you solve problems of misbehavior with your children. Communication will be a key in both cases as we continue to stress the need for participation and mutual respect in handling problems successfully.

First, let's take a look at the "Problem-Handling Model" to get an overview of how this all fits together.

The Problem-Handling Model

The model for handling problems on the next page includes skills presented in this guide.

- It begins with preventing many problems through problem-prevention talks *(Chapter 2)* and family meetings *(Chapters 1-3)*.

- When a problem does occur, determine who owns the problem *(Chapter 1)*.

- If the parent owns the problem , or if it is shared, use discipline skills *(Chapters 2 and 3)*.

- If the child owns the problem, or if it is shared, use support skills *(Chapter 1)*.

- In any of the three cases, you may decide to refer the problem to a family meeting *(Chapters 1-3)*.

- Of course, encouragement is always necessary *(Chapter 3)*.

THE PROBLEM-HANDLING MODEL

Anticipate and prevent problems through Problem-Prevention Talks and Family Meetings
(See Chapters 2 and 3)

If a problem does occur, determine who owns the problem:
(parent, child, or both)

Parent-owned   Shared   Child-owned

Provide discipline.   **Provide discipline and support.**   **Provide support.**

Less Structured Discipline Approaches:
- Polite requests
- "I" messages
- Firm directions

If appropriate, allow natural consequences to teach.

More Structured Discipline Approaches:
- Logical Consequences
- The FLAC Method

Let the child handle the problem, but offer support through active communication.

Refer the problem to a Family Meeting

And no matter who owns the problem: encourage, encourage, encourage!

Who Owns the Problem?

The first step in handling problems that occur in our families is to determine who owns responsibility for handling the problem. With problems due to children's misbehavior, the parent as leader in the family owns responsibility for finding a solution. The discipline skills on the left side of the Problem-Handling Model can be used

The first step in handling problems that occur in our families is to determine who owns responsibility for handling the problem.

to find a solution in these cases. However, there are many problems that children encounter in their lives that are not really our responsibility. These problems are said to be "owned" by the child. When they occur, our job is to offer support using the skills listed on the right side of the model. Sometimes, problems are shared by the parent and the child. In these cases, the parent can offer both support and discipline.

Determining who owns the problem may be a more important part of solving the problem than you might first realize. Children today are very sensitive to their parents trying to run every aspect of their lives. Allowing them the freedom to make decisions, even mistakes, when they own the problem is important in building a cooperative relationship. Dictators take on too many problems as their own. Doormats take on too few. Active parents determine what to do by first determining who owns the problem: themselves or the child. And in some cases they determine that the problem should be shared. In shared situations both discipline and support are often needed.

To help determine who owns a problem, ask yourself the following questions:

? **Who is the problem behavior directly affecting?** Whose needs or goals are being blocked? Who is raising the issue or making the complaint? That person usually owns the problem.

? **Does the problem involve health, safety, or family rules, or values?** If so, then the problem belongs to the parent.

? **Is the problem within reasonable limits for your child's age and level of maturity?** If not, then again, the parent owns responsibility for handling the problem.

Let's look at some examples to help clarify this further.

SITUATION	WHO OWNS the PROBLEM?	Why?
Children are giggling and noisy at a restaurant.	Parent	Parents are eating in a public place and the children's noise is disturbing other patrons and interfering with parents' enjoyment of their meal.
Your child rides her bike on a busy street.	Parent	It is the parents' responsibility to teach their children to use things safely; this situation isn't safe.
Your daughter doesn't like her sister going into her room without asking.	Child	Siblings are entitled to have a relationship with each other without parents interfering. They need to learn to work out together how they can best get along.
Your child complains that the teacher picks on him.	Child	Children have relationships with other adults. They need to learn how to relate to them on their own.
Your child has a temper tantrum in the supermarket.	Parent	The child's behavior is interfering with the parent's goal of shopping.
Your six-year-old complains that he is being picked on by ten-year-olds.	Parent	This would be the child's problem, except that it is beyond his level of maturity to handle.
Your child is not keeping up with his schoolwork.	Shared	The parent's goal of the child being successful in school is blocked, yet school success is also the responsibility of the child.

Notice that last example in the chart is an example of a shared problem. Although schoolwork is the child's responsibility, parents have a right and a responsibility to become involved when the child is not owning this responsibility. The goal in such cases is to shift ownership to the child through both discipline and support methods.

As we move through the next two chapters, we'll learn ways you can support your child when she owns the problem, and also learn effective discipline skills to use when you own the problem. But first, let's talk about an important building block in developing a foundation for either side of the Problem-Handling Model: communication.

Communication: The Road to Cooperation

Many parents have shared that these same communication skills have also made them more effective with coworkers, friends, and even spouses.

Members of a family are all riding in the same boat. Therefore, teaching our kids how to solve problems cooperatively is in all of our interests, and to do so requires first and foremost, good communication skills. The skills that we will be discussing in this chapter are especially useful in helping our children handle problems that they own. However, over the years, many parents have shared that these same communication skills have also made them more effective with coworkers, friends, and even spouses. Why? Because they help build cooperation, which we define like this:

> *Cooperation* **is two or more people working together in a mutually supportive manner for a common goal.**

In a high-tech, diverse, democratic society, the child who learns to work cooperatively with others—to be a team player—has a far greater chance at success than the one who over-emphasizes competition. Ironically, although the ability to compete is certainly valuable in our society, it is the ability to cooperate that makes both individuals and communities great.

Cooperation is a product of both attitude and skills. We can help our children build a cooperative attitude by first developing one in ourselves. We communicate this attitude through our words and actions by treating our children and others respectfully, enforcing reasonable limits, encouraging participation through family meetings and enrichment activities, and working together to solve problems. Building on this foundation, our next step is to develop the communication skills necessary for working together cooperatively. We may want to win cooperation, but without such skills we find the road filled with mistaken signs—or even blocked. The information and skills in the remainder of this chapter will help you put your good intentions into positive action and pave the road ahead with clear, supportive communication.

Mixed Messages

Communication involves much more than just what you say to your child. In fact, your message is carried on three separate channels:

1 **Your words**

2 **Your tone of voice, and**

3 **Your body language, including hand gestures, how close you stand, and facial expressions.**

When it comes to communicating information like a shopping list, your words carry most of the message. However, with emotionally charged messages such as problems, research has shown that more of the message is carried by body language, followed by tone of voice and lastly, the words themselves. In other words, how you say something is often even more important than what you say.

When all three channels of communication carry the same message, the communication is very clear and powerful. However, when we say one thing with our words and something else with our tone and/or body language, we send a mixed message. Mixed messages not only dilute the strength of the message, but are often confusing to the listener.

For example, imagine that your child owns a problem and you have decided to let her handle it. You say, "I'm not angry. You can do whatever you think is best." However, your tone of voice, crossed arms, and scowl all say, "I'll be angry if you don't do what I think is best." This sort of mixed message makes it difficult for your child to know where she stands. An assertive child will probably hear the message she wants to hear and then do what she wants. Other kids, however, may become anxious and confused about what to do. The key is to adjust your attitude so that you really accept her right to make the decision, even if her choice is not what you would prefer. This will reduce your anger, even if you are still somewhat disappointed. You can also change your words to more honestly reflect your feelings.

Example:

> *"I may be disappointed if you decide not to take your sister with you to the playground, but as I said, it's your choice and I can live with it."*
> *(Of course, your face and tone need to communicate this same message.)*

Mixed messages also erode cooperation when the parent owns a problem. For example, you are reading a book when your child asks if he can stay up another hour to watch television. Your words say, "I don't think that's a good idea," but your tone and body language (as you continue to read your book) say, "I'm not really that concerned and if you stay up you probably won't get into trouble."

What do you think your child will do? Like most kids, he will use the confusion to do what he wants to do. Remember, when you split your message you weaken your communication. The clearer you are the more effective you are. Whether using discipline or supporting your child in solving a problem she owns, work to keep your three channels of communication consistent.

Avoiding Communication Blocks

Most parents wish their children would feel freer to come to them with their problems. We want to help them solve these problems and eliminate the pain that such problems can bring. The trouble is that these very problems expose our children's self-esteem like a tender nerve. At such times they are hypersensitive to criticism, negative judgment, and other words or actions that seem to say that they are not worthwhile. If we are fortunate enough to engage a child in talking about a problem, we want to first guard against anything that will block communication and prompt her to withdraw.

A *communication block* is any words, tone of voice or body language that influence a person sharing a problem to end the communication.

Because you communicate your attitude largely through tone of voice and body language, it is not enough just to watch your words. You have to adopt a supportive, nonjudgmental attitude if you are really going to help. When you listen with an attitude of support, your child will begin to trust you with her feelings and share more of what is going on in her life. This sets the stage for you to influence her to make wise decisions. If you jump the gun and block communication, you will have lost this valuable opportunity to offer guidance and win cooperation.

Your goal is not to take over and provide a solution, or to take away your child's pain.

Look at the list of common communication blocks on the next page. Each block ignores the child's thoughts and feelings and instead focuses on the parent's attempt to control the situation. More often than not, these attempts backfire. When people are in pain, they want to know that someone else feels their pain with them. The mistake parents make is launching into an attempt to solve the child's problem instead of offering sympathy or encouragement. Ironically, if you try to solve your child's problems, you will actually diminish her self-esteem. Your goal is not to take over and provide a solution, or to take away your child's pain. It is to offer a caring ear, support, and encouragement, and to help your child find a useful solution for herself.

The first step in helping is to identify your most common pitfalls. Once you are aware that you use them, be on guard the next time your child has a problem, and avoid these pitfalls. When you find yourself using them in the future, catch yourself with a smile—and make a change.

BLOCK	EXAMPLE	PARENT'S INTENTION	WHAT IT REALLY SAYS TO THE CHILD
Commanding	"What you should do is..." "Stop complaining!"	To control the situation. To provide quick solutions.	"You don't have the right to decide how to handle your own problems."
Giving Advice	"I've got a really good idea..." "Why don't you..."	To solve the problem for the child.	"You don't have the good sense to come up with your own solutions."
Placating	"It isn't as bad as it seems" "Everything will be okay."	To take away the child's pain; to make him feel better.	"You don't have a right to your feelings. You can't handle discomfort."
Interrogating	"What did you do to make him..."	To get to the bottom of the problem and find out what the child did wrong.	"You must have messed up somewhere."
Distracting	"Let's not worry about that."	To protect the child from the problem by changing the subject.	"I don't think you can stand the discomfort long enough to find a real solution."
Psychologizing	"Do you know why you said that?" "You're just being oversensitive."	To help prevent future problems by analyzing the child's behavior and explaining his motives.	"I know more about you than you know about yourself. Therefore, I'm superior to you."
Being Judgmental	"Why were you doing that in the first place?" "That wasn't a very smart thing to do."	To help the child realize what she did wrong.	"You have poor judgment. You don't make good decisions."
Sarcasm	"Well, I guess that's just about the end of the world."	To show the child how wrong her attitudes or behavior are by making her feel ridiculous.	"You are ridiculous."
Moralizing	"The right thing to do would be..." "You really should..."	To show the child the proper way to deal with the problem.	"I'll choose your values for you."
Being a Know-It-All	"Everybody knows that when something like this happens, you..."	To show the child that he has a resource for handling any problem—you.	"Since I know it all, you must know nothing."

Active Communication

Instead of blocking communication, you can use "active communication," a set of skills that will help you win cooperation and support your child in solving problems. Active communication is recommended when your child owns a problem you'd like to help her solve, or when you both share responsibility for a problem. There are five steps:

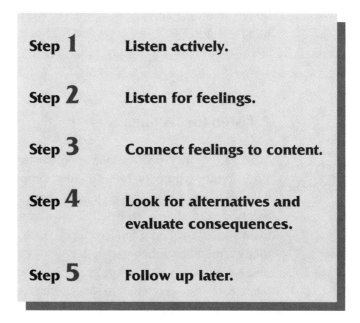

Step 1   **Listen actively.**

Step 2   **Listen for feelings.**

Step 3   **Connect feelings to content.**

Step 4   **Look for alternatives and evaluate consequences.**

Step 5   **Follow up later.**

1. Listen actively.

What do I mean by "active" listening? If you listen fully, you don't just receive information; you are an active participant in the communication process. You listen with your eyes as well as your ears, with your intuition as well as your thinking. With active listening, you're trying to encourage your child to express what he is thinking and feeling. Here's how:

Give full attention. Your child may feel encouraged by the attention alone. It says, "I care about you. You matter. I'm here to help."

Keep your own talk to a minimum. When your mouth is open, your ears don't work as well. So listen, and don't talk a lot.

Acknowledge what you are hearing. Let your child know that you are understanding, that you are taking her words to heart. You can say something as simple as "I see" now and then or even "Uh-huh." Ask questions to clarify what your child is saying or to summarize long stories.

2. Listen for feelings.

Listen to what your child is feeling about her perception of the facts.

Most parents make the mistake of only listening to the content of the child's story. While getting the facts straight is important, it is even more important to listen to what your child is feeling about her perception of the facts. This will help your child acknowledge and accept his feelings rather than keep them bottled up. Some children ignore their painful feelings for so long that they eventually act them out aggressively or suffer from stress-related sickness such as stomachaches or headaches. Part of developing his emotional intelligence is to teach him to say how he feels and then to reflect on his feelings before he decides what action to take.

Until a child has been taught to describe his feelings with words, you will have to listen closely to his tone of voice and watch his face to discover what he is feeling. Then name his feeling in your own mind.

Examples:

> *"This is a really scary situation for Lizzie."*
> *"Raymond sounds really angry."*
> *"She's worried about what the other kids think about her weight."*

Allow yourself to feel some of what your child is feeling.

This type of listening is sometimes called "listening with empathy." **Empathy** means sharing another person's feelings. Allow yourself to feel some of what your child is feeling. This will help you connect with her in a way that shows how much you care, an essential quality in helping someone with an emotionally charged problem. The result of such empathetic listening is usually an increased willingness on the part of the child to continue sharing.

3. Connect feelings to content.

When you have actively listened to what your child has to say and have an idea of what he is feeling, the next step is to reflect those feelings back to him. You can become what psychologist Haim Ginott calls an "emotional mirror." They just reflect what is there. Reflect the feelings and then connect them to what happened—the "content." By responding this way, you communicate the most powerful message of all: You care. Because the content is sometimes obvious, you can often simply respond to the feeling and accomplish the same empathy without sounding like you are repeating what he has just told you.

Examples:

"This storm can be pretty scary, can't it Lizzie?" or
"You seem a little scared, Lizzie."

"You sound really angry that you weren't invited, Raymond." or
"I can hear how angry you are."

"Samantha, you seem worried about what the other kids think about your weight." or
"You seem worried, Samantha."

By reflecting feelings in tentative terms ("It sounds as though…" or "I guess…") you don't come across like you're trying to be a mind-reader or a know-it-all. If you miss your guess about what your child is feeling, she can correct you. That way you're sure you understand what she is saying and feeling.

Example:

> **Samantha:** *No…it's not that. I just don't think they should call me names. It's mean.*
>
> **Mother:** *I see. You're more angry than worried.*

By adjusting to the child's correction, the communication continues to flow.

When you reflect the feeling accurately, an exciting thing will happen. Your child will nod her head in recognition, maybe say "yes," and then continue to share. She will feel understood and cared for—and she may understand herself a little better.

Connecting Feelings to Content

What the Child Says	Feeling Word	What the Parent Says
"Mom, I'm not going to do Jon's dishes again!"	Angry	"You seem angry that I want you to clean all the dishes."
"I missed the foul shot, and we lost the game."	Disappointment	"Sounds like you're really disappointed about that."
"This shirt is so dumb."	Embarrassed	"I guess you're embarrassed about what the other kids will think."
"She invited Caitlyn to her slumber party, but not me!"	Hurt	"Oh, I bet that really hurts your feelings."

4. Look for alternatives and evaluate consequences.

After each alternative that your child comes up with you can help predict the consequences.

Helping children become effective problem solvers is one of the skills that will enable them to survive and thrive in our fast-changing 21st century. Because most children will immediately rush to try whatever solution pops into their minds, our job is to slow them down by helping them look at various options and then predicting the likely consequences of each. You can begin by asking such simple questions as:

> *"What can you do about that?"*
> *"What else could you try?"*

After each alternative that your child comes up with you can help predict the consequences by asking:

> *"What do you think would happen if you did that?"*

It is better for your child to think of alternatives on her own without your prompting. This helps her develop her own problem solving skills and the persistence to keep thinking when solutions do not come easily. It also keeps her from being able to blame you if a solution does not work out well, which strengthens her sense of responsibility. However, when a child cannot

Remember, if the child owns the problem, then your role is that of a helpful consultant.

think of a solution herself, you can sometimes gently suggest some. Be very careful in these cases not to take over or otherwise seem to be insisting that she do it your way. Remember, she owns the problem and your role is that of a helpful consultant who makes suggestions, but does not dictate solutions. You might simply ask, "Would you like to know what others in such a situation have done?"

This is also a good time to use the **"palms up" technique.** By actually turning your palms up and saying, "I don't know what you will decide to do, but what if…," you can leave the final decision in your child's hands. This method lowers resistance and actually allows you to be more of an influence in the long run than if you pointed a finger and said, "Here's what you should do…"

Another non-threatening way of introducing an alternative is through your own self-disclosure. If you faced a similar situation in your own childhood, you can share the story and include any successful solutions that you found.

Example:

> *"That reminds me of a time when I wasn't invited to a party that I really wanted to go to. I sat around feeling hurt for awhile, but then I decided that I wasn't going to let the girl that was giving it ruin my whole day. So I called a friend of mine from another school and we spent the day together having a great time."*

Be careful not to turn this into a lecture of the "when-I-was-child-I walked-five-miles-through-the-snow" type. Remember, too, that your child is free to use or not use your ideas as she thinks best. Unless her solution is unsafe or violates your family values, you have to remain accepting even if she chooses an alternative that you think will fail. After all, she owns the problem. Plus, there is a lot to be learned from failed ideas.

Finally, ask your child what he intends to do, and when. Do this gently, and if he is not ready to commit to a course of action, keep in mind that even Einstein often needed time for ideas to incubate before deciding what to do next.

5. Follow up later.

A tremendous amount is gained by talking about a solution to a problem after it has been tried. Make sure you remember to ask your child how he handled the problem and what kind of results followed. This follow-up not only helps your child learn from the experience, but also validates that your interest was genuine. If the results were good, then a little encouragement is all that is required. However, if the problem still exists, or new ones were created, then you can begin the active communication process all over again to find another solution.

Examples:

> *"How did it go with…?"*
>
> *"Remember that talk we had about _____ the other day? I was wondering how it turned out."*

Putting Active Communication to Work

Now that you are aware of the five steps of the active communication process, look for opportunities to use them to help your child solve her own problems. You'll find that the more supportive you are, the more cooperative your child is likely to be.

If you are having a lot of friction with your child, however, he may not yet be willing to sit down for a long discussion. You can still listen for his feelings and express your empathy.

Examples:

> *"Boy, you sure look down."*
> *"I guess you're really ticked off."*
> *"That must have hurt."*

You can even use this skill when disciplining your child or telling him he can't do something. It may help reduce his anger. Just having his feelings recognized and accepted can sometimes help.

Examples:

> *"I know you're angry that I won't let you stay up later."*
>
> *"I'm sorry my decision feels so bad to you."*
>
> *"If looks could kill, I'd be in real trouble right now."*
>
> *"I can live with you not liking me very much right now, but I don't think I could live with myself if something terrible happened to you."*

Feeling Words

Although the English language has hundreds of words that describe specific feelings, most people do not use many in their daily vocabulary. As you practice looking for the right "feeling words," you will find your feeling word vocabulary increases and the job gets easier. To help with this process, we have included a list of feeling words for you to keep in mind.

WORDS THAT DESCRIBE PLEASANT FEELINGS		WORDS THAT DESCRIBE UNPLEASANT FEELING	
Accepted	Hopeful	Afraid	Jealous
Adequate	Honored	Angry	Let down
Adventurous	Important	Anxious	Lonely
Bold	Joyful	Ashamed	Miserable
Brilliant	Lovely	Bashful	Nervous
Calm	Loving	Bored	Overwhelmed
Caring	Overjoyed	Cautious	Pained
Cheerful	Peaceful	Cheated	Possessive
Comfortable	Peppy	Concerned	Provoked
Confident	Playful	Defeated	Pushed
Content	Pleased	Defiant	Rejected
Daring	Proud	Disappointed	Remorseful
Eager	Refreshed	Discouraged	Resentful
Elated	Relieved	Down	Shy
Encouraged	Satisfied	Embarrassed	Stupid
Energetic	Secure	Envious	Suspicious
Fascinated	Successful	Frustrated	Trapped
Free	Surprised	Guilty	Uncomfortable
Full	Sympathetic	Hateful	Uneasy
Glad	Tranquil	Hesitant	Unhappy
Great	Understood	Hopeless	Unloved
Gutsy	Warm	Hurt	Unsure
Happy	Wonderful	Impatient	Weary
High	Zany	Irritated	Worried

Family Enrichment Activity: Taking Time for Fun

Ever notice that a good salesperson will always spend time developing a positive relationship with you before she tries to sell you anything? She knows that half the job of effectively influencing a person is first developing that relationship. Once the person has been "won over," the sale is much easier. (Can you imagine a salesperson being autocratic and demanding a sale? "You'll buy this because I'm the salesperson and I said so!") The same is true for parenting. The more you can enrich your relationship with your child, the more he will allow you to be an influence in his life. This will prevent many problems as well as make discipline much easier when it is called for.

We will present a Family Enrichment Activity in each chapter. Using these activities, and the other support skills, will strengthen your relationship. If your child is frequently out of control, this may be a way to begin making positive contact. Be creative. Reach out.

The first Family Enrichment Activity is to take time to do something fun with your child. It can be as brief as a few minutes or as long as a day. The key is to make it fun and to try making it a regular part of your relationship. In other words, "Every day a little play." For example:

- *Throw a ball or shoot baskets.*
- *Bake a special dessert together.*
- *Play a game together.*
- *Roughhouse.*
- *Go on an outing ... just the two of you.*
- *Tickle each other.*
- *Tell a joke or funny story.*

To get the most out of this activity:

- *Find activities you both enjoy. Many have little or no cost.*
- *Ask for suggestions from your child, but have some ideas of your own.*
- *Keep it fun! Do not use this time for confrontation.*
- *Record your experiences in your Parent's Guide.*

Family Meetings: Choosing a Family Activity

One of the best ways to prepare your children for success in a democratic society is to teach them the "give and take" that comes with cooperative problem solving or decision making. One excellent way to do this is through family meetings. In each chapter of this guide, I'll suggest a different topic for such a meeting. This week I recommend that you hold a brief family meeting to decide what fun activity your family will choose for a family enrichment activity for this week. Keep the meeting

informal and brief, so that nobody comes to resent the forum. To keep the meeting running smoothly, start by suggesting one basic ground rule for family meetings, asking if everyone will agree to the following:

>*We will treat each other
>   respectfully.*

Next, ask everyone to contribute some ideas about what that means to them, and list these ideas for future reference. For example:

>*We will listen while someone else is speaking.*
>*We will wait until the speaker is finished before speaking ourselves.*
>*We will not insult or put down anybody else's ideas.*

By getting agreement for these basic ground rules now, you will have the ability to refer to it later whenever someone acts disrespectfully during a meeting. All you need say is, "Remember our agreement to act respectfully during our meetings?" If this reminder is not enough, you can add the specific violation. For example, "We agreed not to talk when someone else is talking." You may also want to post the ground rules where all family members can review them from time to time.

Be careful, however, not to turn the meeting into one of confrontation. Your goal is to establish family meetings as enjoyable times that allow children to have their voices heard and their wishes considered. Stay upbeat and encouraging as much as possible and you will find that family meetings are a great benefit to parents and children alike.

A Final Thought: Expressing love.

Building a positive relationship with children is an ongoing process, and it sometimes takes steady effort. As we have seen, it involves making arrangements to have fun together, using active communication, and showing mutual respect. Most of all, the positive relationship between parent and child involves expressing love for each other. All children hunger for love, even those who make a career of acting "unlovable." Children need to know that whatever else may happen, their parents love them. Methods of expressing love to children can be woven into the fabric of everyday life: a kiss, a pat on the back, a tousling of hair, an arm around the shoulder. But it is equally important to be able to say to your child that you love him. The words may come awkwardly for some parents. But the important thing is how beautiful they sound to children.

Parents can say, "I love you" when the child will be surprised at the timing, but pleased with the message. Parents can say "I love you" at a time of calmness or tenderness, such as bedtime, and the child can bask in the warmth of the words. For example:

"I love you.

Home Activities

Make an effort to put the ideas and skills you are learning to work. The Home Activities will help.

The best way to learn any new skill—from riding a bike, to learning how to use a computer, to new parenting techniques—is to practice, practice, practice. And the more you practice, the more positive the outcome.

At the end of each chapter, you'll find a list of home activities. These activities are designed to help you practice the ideas and skills presented in the chapter. During the next week, make an effort to put these ideas to work, and record your experiences on the worksheets found at the end of this guide as indicated.

Chapter 1

HOME ACTIVITIES

- **Practice giving choices to your child, and complete the worksheet on page 124.**
- **Complete the Communication Blocks chart on page 126.**
- **Practice Active Communication when your child owns a problem, and fill out the guidesheet on page 130.**
- **Have a Family Meeting about "taking time for fun," and record your results on page 131.**
- **Don't expect your kids to change this week!**

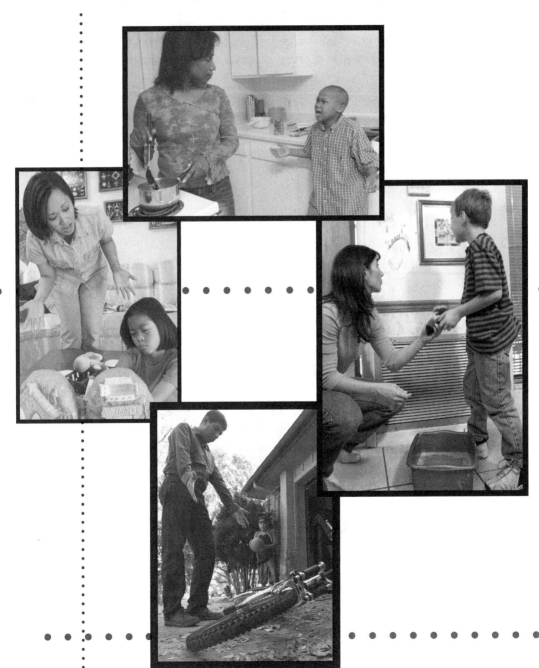

This chapter and the next will present discipline skills for handling problems and misbehavior when they occur in a family. But this chapter is also about something much more basic to the development of a child's ability to thrive in our modern society. It is about **responsibility**.

What is Responsibility?

Everyone talks about responsibility, but what does the word really mean? Let's consider three definitions:

> **Responsibility means:**
>
> **1. Accepting one's obligations.**
>
> **2. Doing the right thing as the situation calls for it.**
>
> **3. Accepting accountability for one's actions.**

Responsibility Means Accepting One's Obligations

Teaching our children that there are times when we must sacrifice our own short-term desires for long-term benefits is teaching them responsibility.

There are times in all of our lives when we would rather not do some things that we feel obligated to do. These "obligations" are sometimes specifically made between two people. For example, when you tell your child that you will pick her up after school, you are obligated to be there. Other obligations are made implicitly through the roles we accept in our daily lives. The job of parenting, for example, carries with it many obligations including providing food, clothing, shelter, discipline, and support. Teaching our children that there are times when we must sacrifice our own short-term desires for long-term benefits is teaching them responsibility. Childhood is filled with opportunities to teach this lesson.

Examples:

- *Owning a pet means accepting responsibility for caring for it.*
- *Being on a team means showing up for practice and games.*
- *Learning a musical instrument means practicing.*
- *Being in a family means doing chores.*
- *Being a student means doing homework and studying.*

Responsibility Means
Doing the Right Thing as the Situation Calls for It

Helping our children learn the difference between right and wrong and instilling the desire to do what is right even when it is difficult or painful, is one of the more challenging jobs of parenthood. We want our children to grow up to be good people who do right things, but often what is right is difficult to know. Sometimes doing the right thing even conflicts with the law, as was the case during the civil rights movement. At other times, the population as a whole is split about what is right and what is wrong, as in the case of abortion. Your own family values and faith will have to guide you in many such situations.

Doing the right thing is often a lot like spelling. For every rule there seems to be an exception.

Examples:

- *Do not hurt someone...unless it's in self-defense.*
- *Do not lie…unless it's a white lie to spare feelings.*
- *Work hard…but don't be a workaholic.*
- *Stand up for your friends…unless they are doing something wrong.*

Taking time to talk with your children about real life situations is the best way to help them grapple with the many nuances of right and wrong. Asking them, "What do you think is the right thing to do?" implies that in your family you strive to know what is right and to do it. When your child does the right thing, be sure to encourage her by acknowledging both the action and the courage it took to act.

Responsibility Means
Accepting Accountability for One's Actions

At the very core of responsibility is accepting that what happens to us results from decisions that we make.

At the very core of responsibility is accepting that what happens to us results from decisions that we make. It is much easier for children, as well as adults, to blame their problems on other people or circumstances, or to just make excuses. But doing so prevents them from learning how to make better decisions in the future. After all, if it wasn't their fault why should they bother to think about what they could do differently next time?

Learning to accept responsibility helps children become very creative at solving problems. Such children grow into adults who are constantly examining life and finding ways to make it work better. They become successful adults who, when they do make a mistake, accept the consequences, learn from it, and then move on. Those who never learn this lesson in responsibility often go through life making the same mistakes over and over.

Responsibility ➡ Growth ➡ Success Cycles

Why do we avoid responsibility if this is so? Because we are afraid of being blamed or punished for making mistakes. Who would blame or punish us? Sometimes it is critical people with whom we live or work. But even their criticism would be harmless if it were not for the fact that we blame and punish ourselves the most.

Where did we learn this self-criticism? Most of us learned it a long time ago from our parents, many of whom believed in the autocratic or permissive methods of parenting and the blame and criticism that went with these styles.

How do we avoid responsibility? We blame others for our mistakes and failures, or we blame circumstances, because it is too painful to accept responsibility and suffer the self-criticism we often heap on ourselves.

We say, "You made me late," or "You made me angry." Or we justify our failings: "Being late isn't such a big deal;" "I have a bad temper;" "I'm a Leo;" "I'm an alcoholic;" "I'm just no good;" "Nobody told me not to."

How can we help prepare children for responsible adulthood? The first step is for us to resist the temptation to blame and punish them for their mistakes and misbehavior. These techniques actually influence them to avoid responsibility—to blame and justify. This chapter is about other methods of disciplining children, methods that teach responsibility while they help you handle everyday problems. But first, let's look at the circumstances in which choices are made.

Freedom and the Limits to Freedom

Responsibility requires that a person be held accountable for his choices, but a choice can be made only when there is freedom to choose. For if the person is not free to choose, we have to assume that someone else has already made the choice for the person. An essential condition for responsibility, therefore, is the freedom to choose.

Without structure and limits, children do not learn responsibility.

Dictator parents give their children almost no freedom to make choices. They believe that since children lack experience, parents must make choices for them. They may want to help their children avoid the pain and pitfalls of poor choices. However, these parents stifle their child's ability to handle responsibility. The child eventually rebels against these strict limits, and yet remains inexperienced at making choices on his own. The results are the very pain and pitfalls the parent sought to avoid.

Doormat parents follow a model of parenting that resembles lawlessness. Such parents allow their children too much freedom to choose. Yet without structure and limits, children do not learn responsibility any better in these circumstances than in an autocratic home.

> *A young man executed in the electric chair for the murder of a woman and her three small children reported that he would probably do it again if he had the chance, because he came from a home where no one ever told him not to do certain things. He had grown up without limits—free to do whatever he pleased. And was he happy about this? Hardly. He chose the electric chair instead of imprisonment because he described his life as a "living hell."*

So children clamor for freedom to make their own choices while parents call for limits to that freedom, and the dialogue becomes a universal chant, repeated the world over:

"Freedom!" "Limits." **"FREEDOM!" "LIMITS!"**

Fortunately, there is a third alternative—"active" parenting. Active parents are acutely aware of their children's need for freedom, but freedom within well-defined limits. They work hard to set limits in line with each child's age and level of responsibility. They are aware that over-restrictive limits lead to sneaking around and other forms of rebellion, and too-loose limits lead to selfish and destructive behavior.

Freedom Within Limits

This concept of "freedom within expanding limits" suggests that a three-year-old will make fewer of her own decisions than a ten-year-old, who again will make fewer decisions than a 17-year-old. In fact, the ideal situation for a teen spending her last year at home is for her to make almost all

Active parents are acutely aware of their children's need for freedom, but freedom within well-defined limits.

of her own decisions. The parent has become almost like a roommate and consultant. This makes sense when we consider that our goal is to prepare children for independent living, because we won't always be around to provide limits.

Like most things, teaching responsibility is a gradual process. It involves giving children choices and then allowing them to experience the consequences of those choices. In fact, since responsibility is a matter of accepting the consequences of our choices, then a reasonable formula for teaching responsibility to children is:

Responsibility = Choice + Consequence

What are our best opportunities for using this formula? First, we can let the child make more daily decisions. We can allow increasing freedom to make such choices as what to eat and what to wear, keeping in mind the child's age and stage of development. (Refer to "The Method of Choice" section in Chapter One on page 27.) Second, when we have a problem with the child's behavior, we can look for opportunities to give her choices and allow her to experience the consequences of her actions. This combination of choice and consequence, as we will see later in this chapter, is a very effective discipline method.

Reward and Punishment Often Backfire

Discipline is important for teaching most children how to live within the limits of the situation and the values of the family. However, discipline does not necessarily mean reward and punishment. In fact, the word itself comes from the Latin word, disciplina, which means "to teach." How we choose to teach our children right from wrong, the importance of fulfilling their obligations, and accepting responsibility for their actions can be for better or for worse.

We mentioned earlier that reward and punishment are how the dictator parent enforces his orders. Children are kept in line with the threat of punishment if they misbehave and the promise of reward if they do what the parent wants them to do. This system of reward and punishment may have been effective in older days when the world was ruled by kings, queens, and emperors and everyone "knew his place," but in a society of equals, it doesn't work very well.

REWARD: **something extra that is thrown in to bribe the child to change behavior.**

For one thing, a reward for good behavior comes to be expected almost as a right. A child does not learn to behave cooperatively just because the situation calls for it, or because the family functions better when everyone follows the rules or pitches in. Instead, he develops a "what's in it for me" attitude that leads him to expect more and more rewards for positive behavior. The parent must then increase the value of the reward to keep it effective until she reaches a point of frustration. This frustration often leads to the use of punishment.

INCENTIVE: **built into the sequence of events on a regular basis and is logically connected.**

In a society of equals, when you hurt someone, you give that person an unspoken right to hurt you back.

On the other hand, incentives, when used correctly as part of a logical consequence, can be very effective because, unlike rewards, they are logically connected to the situation. We'll learn more about using incentives as part of When/Then choices later in this chapter.

Punishment continues to be a popular method for many parents because it does appear to work in the short run. Under the threat of punishment children will often improve negative behavior. However, punishment is not effective in the long run because it often creates resentment on the part of the child. In a society of equals, when you hurt someone, you give that person an unspoken right to hurt you back. Children will usually find ways of getting even through future misbehavior or worse.

In fact, reward and punishment are out of place among equals. It is only a superior who can give rewards and mete out punishments, and it is only inferiors who can receive them. All in all, rewards and punishments as methods of child-rearing are holdovers from an earlier time when the world was a different place. There are much more effective methods of discipline, and we will become acquainted with them in this program.

Effective Discipline and the Problem-Handling Model

We discussed in Chapter One the importance of using problems as teaching tools for instilling qualities of character such as cooperation, courage, and responsibility in children. Let's refer again to the Problem-Handling Model that was presented in that chapter and notice the highlighted areas. These include methods of preventing problems, and then how to handle problems that the parent owns using effective discipline. The remainder of this chapter will focus on how to use these powerful skills to teach your child responsibility and how to live within the limits that you determine as the leader in the family.

THE PROBLEM-HANDLING MODEL

Anticipate and prevent problems through Problem-Prevention Talks and Family Meetings
(See Chapters 2 and 3)

If a problem does occur, determine who owns the problem:
(parent, child, or both)

Parent-owned

Shared

Child-owned

Provide discipline.

Provide discipline and support.

Provide support.

Less Structured Discipline Approaches:
- Polite requests
- "I" messages
- Firm directions

If appropriate, allow natural consequences to teach.

More Structured Discipline Approaches:
- Logical Consequences
- The FLAC Method

Let the child handle the problem, but offer support through active communication.

Refer the problem to a Family Meeting

And no matter who owns the problem: encourage, encourage, encourage!

Effective Discipline

Of course, we won't be able to prevent all problems. At times children will become discouraged and turn to negative behavior to achieve their goals. When misbehavior occurs, discipline is often required to motivate the child to change behavior. When using any of the discipline skills that will follow, keep in mind these tips:

1. **Our goal is to teach our children, not to hurt them.** In fact, we can teach far better without hurting their feelings or their bottoms.

2. **Whenever we discipline a child for negative behavior, we want to find opportunities to encourage any improvement the child makes.**

3. **When using discipline to influence our children, we always want to use the least assertive method that will work.**

4. **Let discipline be motivated by caring.** When a child knows that you are disciplining her because you care about her, it's easier to accept. When we discipline out of frustration, anger, and our own desires, it's difficult for the child to accept or "learn" the lesson we're trying to teach.

The first three discipline methods that we will present are basic communication methods that increase in assertiveness from mild to firm. Begin with the first, and if it does not work move on to the second, and then the third. They are:

- **Polite Requests**

- **"I" Messages**

- **Firm reminders**

Polite Requests

Not every problem or conflict requires a full-fledged discussion or firm discipline. As we said before, sometimes the reason a child misbehaves is simply because they do not know what you expect of them. Often, a polite request is enough to influence a child to change behavior (especially if the relationship is already a positive one).

The first step is to politely make our desires known through a request.

The first step is to politely make our desires known through a request. For example, you have decided that you no longer want to pamper your child by picking up the dirty dishes he leaves in the den. Your polite request might be:

> *"Honey, from now on will you do me a favor and bring your dishes to the sink when you're through with your snack?"*

If your child agrees, be sure to add:

> *"Thanks, that will be a big help."*

This may seem too obvious to mention, but we parents do talk to children in ways that would be clearly disrespectful if used with other adults. The parent in the above example could easily wait until she is fed up with being a servant, hold it inside for another week to let it really boil, then burst out with "I'm sick and tired of having to pick up your mess! What do you think I am, your personal servant? If you weren't so lazy and inconsiderate ..." This kind of outburst is not likely to produce responsibility, cooperation—or dishes in the sink.

If a child does comply with our polite request, but slips up, we can offer a friendly reminder:

> *"Honey, I notice you forgot to put your dishes in the sink. Please come get them."*

When a child repeatedly forgets to keep an agreement, then a stronger communication is called for.

"I" Messages

"I" messages, a term coined by the late psychologist Thomas Gordon, are firm and calm communications that can produce surprisingly effective results. They are called "I" messages because they shift the emphasis from the child (a traditional "you" message) to how the parent ("I") feels about the child's behavior. "I" Messages:

- **Allow the parent to say how he or she feels about the child's behavior without blaming or labeling the child.**

- **Create a situation in which the child is more likely to hear what the parent is saying because it is expressed in a nonthreatening way.**

- **Convey clearly to the child one consequence (the parent's feeling) of the child's behavior.**

- **Put the emphasis on the child's behavior and not on the child's personality.**

- **Give the child clear information about what change in behavior the parent wants.**

When To Use an "I" Message:

When a polite request has failed to change behavior, an "I" message is a more assertive next step.

"I" messages are only effective when the parent owns the problem. When a polite request has failed to change behavior, an "I" message is a more assertive next step.

Since "I" messages work best in a firm and calm tone of voice, avoid using them when you are too angry. Allow for a cooling-off period, then approach your child when you have regained control. An angry "I" message can easily trigger rebellion in a power-seeking child.

How To Send an "I" Message:

There are four parts to an "I" message.

1. Name the behavior or situation you want changed. In order to avoid attacking a child's self esteem it is important to "separate the deed from the doer" It isn't that the child is bad, only that we have a problem with something the child is doing. By beginning with a statement aimed at the behavior, we avoid attacking the child's personality and self-esteem. We begin with "I have a problem with ..." For example:

"I have a problem with your leaving dirty dishes on the coffee table."

2. Say how you feel about the situation. This lets the child know that the problem is serious to you (without raising your voice). Although parents often use the word "angry" to describe their feelings, this is often a mask for two other emotions: "fear" and "hurt." Children can usually hear us better when we are expressing these emotions because they are less threatening. "I feel concerned" or "I feel hurt" may be closer to the truth, as well as more effective. This part of the "I" message begins with "I feel..." For example:

"I feel taken advantage of... "

3. State your reason. Nobody likes to be treated as if he were expected to be blindly obedient. If we are going to change what is comfortable to us to please an authority, we at least want that authority to have a good reason. Children are no exception. A simple explanation about how the child's behavior is interfering with your needs or the needs of the situation can go a long way. For example:

"... because I have to spend time and energy cleaning up behind you."

Remember, you get more of what you ask for than what you don't ask for.

4. Say what you want done. You have already made a polite request or two, so now you are getting more assertive. This means letting your child know exactly what you would like done. Remember, you get more of what you ask for than what you don't ask for. This step can begin with "I want" or "I would like." For example:

> *"I would like you to bring your dirty dishes to the kitchen and put them in the dishwasher when you leave the den."*

Putting this "I" message all together, we have:

> *"I have a problem with your leaving dirty dishes on the coffee table. I feel taken advantage of because I have to spend time and energy cleaning up behind you. I would like you to bring your dirty dishes to the kitchen and put them in the dishwasher when you leave the den."*

Making "I" Messages Stronger: Two Variations

1. Getting agreement. "Will you please ..." We can make an "I" message even stronger by getting an agreement from the child about the behavior we want changed. This can be done by simply adding the question, "Will you do that?" and then not moving until you get a "yes." Saying "yes" verbally commits the child to action and helps motivate her to follow through later. This can also be done by changing the last step of the "I" message from "I would like ..." to "Will you please ..." For example:

> *"I have a problem with your leaving dirty dishes on the coffee table. I feel taken advantage of because I have to spend time and energy cleaning up behind you. Will you please bring your dirty dishes to the kitchen and put them in the dishwasher when you are finished? Will you do that?"*

2. Establishing a time frame. "When?" Every parent knows the frustrations of getting an agreement from a child about doing something, finding it still not done hours later, and confronting the child only to hear the refrain, "I'll do it." The implication, of course, is "I'll do it when I get around to it," and that may not occur in this decade.

The solution is to get a clear agreement as to when the behavior will be completed. In the above example, the "when" is built into the phrase "when you are finished." Other times, it can be added right after the child agrees to the request by simply asking, "When?"

Firm Directions

If your child does not respond to a polite request or an "I" Message, your next step is to give a short, but firm, reminder. By suspending the rules of grammar and syntax, you give the message additional "oomph."

Example:

"Dishes. Sink. Now."

The fewer words you use the better. This means avoiding the temptation to give a mini lecture on responsibility while your child sits there ignoring you. Just make solid eye-contact and firmly remind your child about what you want done.

Make solid eye-contact and firmly remind your child about what you want done.

Your child may very well spring into action, amazing you and surprising himself in the process. If so, build on this success, as always by encouraging him with a thank-you. However, some kids seem to need a lot of reminders, in which case it may be time to move on to the more advanced discipline methods: the rack and the screw. (Just kidding! These methods have been replaced in this edition with logical consequences and the FLAC Method.)

Logical Consequences

In order to influence a child to change from a negative behavior to a positive one, the child first needs clear information from the parent about what change is expected. The basic discipline methods just covered provide the clear, firm communication to do this. However, children sometimes need to experience a more concrete consequence of their actions in order to learn the lesson of responsibility. Remember:

Responsibility = Choice + Consequence

Consequences are powerful teachers about the effectiveness of our choices and behavior.

We have already seen how reward and punishment as consequences can often backfire. The use of logical consequences offers an advanced form of discipline that is more consistent with life in a modern democratic society. A logical consequence can be defined like this:

> *Discipline that is logically connected to a misbehavior and applied by an authority to influence a child to behave within the limits of the situation.*

Consequences are powerful teachers about the effectiveness of our choices and behavior. Better than a punishment or lecture, consequences offer parents their prime discipline tools. There are two types of consequences: natural consequences and logical consequences. We'll cover natural consequences in Chapter Three. For now we'll concentrate on logical consequences.

Examples:

> *When Sean continues to forget to bring his dirty dishes into the kitchen after snacking in the den, he loses the privilege of taking food out of the kitchen.*
>
> *When Carly refuses to put away her toys, her mother puts them in the closet, out of reach, for the next day.*
>
> *When Dennis The Menace® uses crayon on the wall, he must use his time and energy to wash it off.*

Born Again

Dennis the Menace ® used by permission of Hank Ketchum and © by North American Syndicate.

Logical Consequences Vs. Punishment

Logical consequences are not the same thing as punishment, even though the child will usually experience both as unpleasant. Some of the differences include:

LOGICAL CONSEQUENCES	PUNISHMENT
are logically connected to the misbehavior	is an arbitrary retaliation for misbehavior
are intended to teach responsible behavior	is intended to teach blindly obedient behavior
are administered in a firm and calm manner	is often delivered in an atmostphere of anger and resentment
are respectful	is disrespectful
allow the child to participate	is dictated by the authority

Types of Logical Consequences: Either/Or and When/Then Choices

Learning how to handle responsibility is learning how to make good decisions. Logical consequences should therefore always be presented in the form of a choice. The consequences of children's choices teach them how to make better choices in the future. Parents can help children in this learning process by showing them that misbehavior is one of their choices, but that it brings with it logical consequences. It should also be emphasized to the child that a positive choice will bring about positive consequences.

There are two types of choices you will find extremely useful:

- **Either-or choices: "Either you may ... or you may ... You decide."**

- **When-then choices: "When you have ... then you may ..."**

Either/Or Choices

Either/or choices are particularly effective when you want your child to stop a misbehavior:

> (Katherine leaves her belongings scattered around the kitchen in the afternoon.) *"Katherine, either put your things away when you come home from school, or I'll put them in a box in the basement. You decide."*

Notice that the logical consequence of leaving her belongings lying around is the inconvenience of having to dig them out of a junk box in the basement.

> (Calvin continues to forget to put his dirty clothes in the hamper.) *"Calvin, either put your dirty clothes in the hamper, or wash them yourself. You decide."*

The logical consequence of not putting his dirty clothes in the hamper is that he must do his own wash.

When/Then Choices

When/then choices are effective when you want to motivate your child to start a behavior:

> (Maria has trouble getting her homework done but likes to spend time chatting online with her friends.) *"Maria, when you have finished your homework, then you may go online.*

Notice that the logical consequence of not doing her homework is losing the privilege of using the computer. However, by phrasing the consequence positively, as a when/then choice, the options are more attractive to the child and she is more likely to be motivated to finish the homework.

(Tom is about to go play in the backyard, ignoring his regular Saturday chore of cleaning his room.) *"Tom, when you have cleaned your room, then you may go play outside."*

It is easy to accidentally turn a logical consequence into a punishment.

It is easy to accidentally turn a logical consequence into a punishment. The following examples are poorly expressed because they are couched in negative terms: "Don't do that or else..." They can easily be seen as punishment—especially when accompanied by a harsh tone of voice and aggressive body language.

Poor:

> *"Katherine, put your things away or I'm going to throw them in a box in the basement!"*
>
> *"Calvin, if you don't start putting your dirty clothes in the hamper, you're going to have to wash them yourself."*
>
> *"Tom, you may not go play outside until you have cleaned your room."*

Guidelines for Using Logical Consequences

The following guidelines will help ensure that you are really using logical consequences and not punishment. They may seem like a lot to remember, but as you practice using them they will become second nature.

1. Ask the child to help set the consequences. Since life in our democratic society requires the participation of all those concerned with a problem, we stand a much better chance that a child will cooperate with our authority if we include her in the decision-making process. You may be surprised how often the child will come up with choices and solutions that we wouldn't have thought of alone. For example:

> *"Katherine, I still have a problem with you leaving your belongings all over the kitchen. What do you think we can do to solve it?"*

One key to the success of logical consequences is that the consequence is logically connected to the misbehavior.

Even if the child has no helpful suggestions or is uncooperative about finding a solution, the important thing is that you asked. Since you have invited the child's participation, she will be less likely to think of you as a dictator and to rebel against your authority. Of course, you will want to come to the discussion prepared with your own logical consequences in case your child has no ideas.

2. Give the child a choice. If the child has a choice in the matter, she is much more likely to choose the positive behavior. Use either/or and when/then choices. Remember, either/or choices work well when you want to stop a misbehavior, and when/then choices are useful when you want to encourage a positive behavior.

3. Make sure the consequences are really logical. One key to the success of logical consequences is that the consequence is logically connected to the misbehavior. Children are better able to see the justice of such consequences and will usually accept them without resentment. However, if the consequence you select is not really related to the child's behavior, it will come across as a punishment.

Not Logical:

"Either come in to dinner when I call or no TV for a week."

"Either play quietly while I work or I'm not taking you to the movie we planned."

"Either stop fighting or you'll both get a spanking."

Logical:

"Either come in to dinner when I call or it will get cold—and you may miss it altogether."

"When it gets quiet enough for me to finish my work, then I'll continue so that we'll be able to make the movie."

"Either stop fighting or you'll have to play in separate rooms."

4. Only give choices you can live with. There are many potential logical consequences for any given problem. For that reason, brainstorming with other parents, a spouse, or even the child can help. However, when you own the problem, it is up to you to decide which choices to give your child. Only give choices you as a parent can accept.

For example, if your child continues to forget to put his dishes in the dishwasher, a choice might be:

> *"Either put your dishes in the dishwasher, or I'll leave them in the sink and there will be no clean dishes."*

However, if you know a sink full of dirty dishes will drive you crazy, then don't give him this choice. Why? Because you will likely sabotage the consequences by getting angry as the dishes pile up. In addition, your own values and desires are important. It is much better to keep thinking until you can come up with a consequence that won't punish you. For example:

> *"Either put your dirty dishes in the dishwasher or hire me as your waitress to do it for you."*
> *"Either put your dirty dishes in the dishwasher, or I will serve the next meal without dishes."*

By the way, parents who have used the above consequence say it takes only one meal of spaghetti eaten off a bare table by hand to teach the lesson. However, once again, if you couldn't live with the mess, then don't give this particular choice. What works for one family may not be acceptable for another.

It is essential that you remain both firm and calm.

5. Keep your tone firm and calm. When giving the choice, as well as later when you enforce the consequence, it is essential that you remain both firm and calm. An angry tone of voice (the dictator's pitfall) invites rebellion and a fight. On the other hand, a wishy-washy tone of voice (the doormat's pitfall) suggests to the child that you don't really mean what you say. This invites noncompliance. In a democratic society, a firm and calm tone used by an authority figure says, " I recognize that you have a right to be treated respectfully, but you are out-of-bounds here. My job is to help you learn to stay in bounds, and I plan to do my job."

6. Give the choice one time, then act to enforce the consequence. For a logical consequence to teach a lesson, it must be enforced. If the child continues to choose to misbehave, then immediately follow through with the consequences. One way or another, children always choose. Even if they don't respond verbally, their behavior will tell you what choice has been made. Do not give the choice a second time without putting the consequences into effect immediately. The child must see that the choice results in a consequence, and the lesson must be clear, or the value is diminished. For example:

> *"If your books were in the kitchen when I cleaned, then you will find them in the junk box in the basement."*

The child is actually testing to see if we will really do what we say we will do.

7. Expect testing. When you attempt to redirect a child's misbehavior from negative choices towards positive ones, expect her to continue to misbehave for a while. We call this testing, because the child is actually testing to see if we will really do what we say we will do. In other words, will we change our behavior? Whether we realize it or not, she was getting some pay-off from our

old way of responding, and she will likely try to get us to revert to what we usually do. Even a punishment, as we will see in the next chapter, can have a hidden pay off. The active parent will therefore expect that the child may continue to misbehave for awhile as a test of our commitment to change the game. If we consistently enforce the consequences, she will soon see that her testing isn't working and will change her behavior. After all, children don't continue doing what doesn't work.

8. Allow the child to try again after experiencing the consequences. Since the goal is for the child to learn from the consequences of his choice, opportunities must be provided to try again—but only after the child has experienced the logical consequence. For example, Tom has agreed that when he has cleaned his room on Saturdays, then he may go play outside. Dad sees Tom heading out the back door before the room is cleaned and reminds him of his obligation.

If the child repeats the misbehavior after experiencing the consequences, then he may be testing. One can meet this challenge by letting the consequences operate a little longer after the second try, and longer yet after the third. For example, if Tom starts heading outside again next week without doing his chores, Dad can say:

> *"It seems that you have decided not to play outside this morning Take care of your room and we can try again this afternoon."*

Logical Consequences Guidelines

1. Ask the child to help

2. Give the child a choice.

- Either/Or Choice

- When/Then Choice.

3. Make sure the consequence is logical.

4. Give choices you can live with.

5. Keep your tone firm and calm.

6. Give the choice one time, then act.

7. Expect testing.

8. Allow the child to try again later.

Family Meeting: Problem-Prevention Talk

Many conflicts and misunderstandings can be prevented if we will take the time to discuss guidelines and expectations before the situation occurs.

Children often misbehave simply because they don't know what we expect from them. In other words, they don't know where the limits are and how much freedom they are allowed. Of course, many a shrewd child will intentionally stay in the dark about the rules, operating on the belief that "it is easier to gain forgiveness than permission." In either case, many conflicts and misunderstandings can be prevented if we will take the time to discuss guidelines and expectations before the situation occurs.

As the parent you will have certain limits that are non-negotiable.

Problem prevention is not about laying down the law or telling your child about your guidelines. You will find that you can be much more effective if you will discuss potential problems together and decide on the needs of the situation. Of course, as the parent you will have certain limits that are non-negotiable, but a willingness to be flexible within those limits can go a long way to winning cooperation and avoiding problems.

Example:

> *You have decided to take your five-year-old grocery shopping with you. Talking with her before you leave home can improve your chances for having a problem-free outing and may save you a lot of time—and stress—in the store.*

Here are some tips for such a prevention discussion:

1. **Identify potential problems and risks.** If you have been in similar situations before, then you probably know where the trouble spots will be. Otherwise, use your experience of similar situations and your knowledge of your child to anticipate the problems.

For example, your child often whines for a toy whenever you are in a store. He also has a tendency to wander off, forcing you to chase after him.

2. **Share thoughts and feelings.** Ask your child what he thinks about the situation and what problems might arise. You may be surprised that he also has concerns. Then make clear your own thoughts and feelings in a friendly manner.

For example, your child may feel that shopping is boring and he'd rather be outside playing. You might say that you understand that shopping is boring for him, but that you need to buy food for the family to eat.

Talk with your child about what is expected.

3. **Generate guidelines for behavior** (making the situation a win-win for both of you.) Using the information you gathered in step two, talk with your child about what is expected. When discussing guidelines, keep in mind that it is easier to comply with the rules if you enjoy the situation. We aren't suggesting the use of rewards or bribes for cooperative behavior, but rather to include some incentives.

For example, avoid:

> *"If you'll be good, I'll buy you a toy."* This is a bribe or a reward, and will lead to having to buy the child something every time you go to the store.

Better:

> *"If we get our shopping done on time, we'll have time to stop by the park on the way home."*

Best:

> *"How would you like to help me do the shopping by handing me the groceries off the shelf? Maybe you can help me decide some things you'd like to have for dinner."*
>
> *"Great! I also need for you to stay beside me all the time so that you'll be safe and we won't interfere with other shoppers."*

For more challenging kids, however, consequences are very helpful when done right.

4. Decide on logical consequences for violating the guidelines (if necessary). Your child will be more likely to follow the guidelines if he knows what will happen if he violates a guideline. You don't need to use this step with children who are basically cooperative or who have not had problems in similar situations. In fact, such a warning may seem like an insult to a child who only needs to be included in the discussion and have his needs considered in order to cooperate. For more challenging kids, however, consequences are very helpful when done right.

For example:

> *When we get to the store you will either need to stay with me or else I'll have to put you in the cart.*

5. Follow-up later. In situations in which you are not around to ensure that the guidelines were followed, you will need to check up to see how your child behaved. If she has followed the guidelines then you can encourage her by acknowledging the good effort. If she has not, then you will need to enforce the logical consequences.

For example:

> *Karen, we agreed that you would put away your toys before dinner or else I would take them away for two days. I just want to let you know that you can have your toys back on Monday.*

Family Enrichment Activity: Positive "I" Messages.

We saw earlier in this chapter that "I" messages offer parents an effective way to confront their children about repeated misbehavior. They are clear, firm, calm communications that are often easy for children to hear without becoming defensive. These same features also make it possible to use "I" messages as encouraging statements when children are behaving well. Positive "I" messages, as we call them, can help motivate a child to continue improving her behavior.

For example, we saw how Dennis the Menace's mother used a logical consequence to teach her son not to paint on the walls. Let's say she "catches him being good" and wants to offer some encouragement. She can use a positive "I" message like this:

1. **State what you like.**
   "I really like the way you are using paper for your art project."

2. **Say how you feel.**
   "I feel good knowing that you heard what I said about the walls…"

3. **Tell them why.**
   "…because now we can have clean walls and some creative art work."

4. **Offer to do something for him**.
   "How about if we tape your picture over here like a painting in a museum?"

You may have noticed that this fourth step is slightly different than with the other "I" message. When we use an "I" message to discipline, the fourth step is to tell the child the behavior change that we want. Now that we have that change, we want to encourage his effort by making it a win/win. Just make sure that this doesn't become a reward. It will help to keep the offer logically connected to their positive behavior as Dennis's mother did in the previous example. You might even think of this as a "positive logical consequence." For example:

After using "I" messages and logical consequences to decrease the fighting between your children, you catch them cooperating. At the end of your positive "I" message, you let them know that their cooperation has let you get your work done faster so now you have time to make some popcorn, play with them, or teach them how to play a new game.

Don't worry if you don't use every step of the positive "I" message every time. The first statement alone (telling them what you like) is a good use of encouragement by itself. And feel free to use your own words so that the message feels natural to you.

Chapter 2

HOME ACTIVITIES

- Practice using polite requests, "I" messages, and firm directions, and fill out the worksheet on page 132.

- Practice using a Logical Consequence and complete the worksheet on page 134.

- Have a Problem-Prevention Talk to address a potential problem in your family. Fill in the worksheet on page 135.

- Family Enrichment Activity: Use a positive "I" message to encourage your child's improvement or other positive behavior, and complete the worksheet on page 136.

Chapter 3
Power, Courage, and Self-Esteem

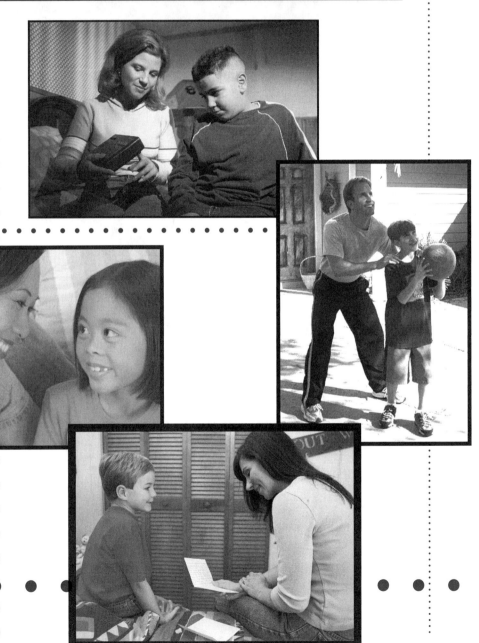

The first time I was a guest on the Oprah Winfrey Show, Oprah asked me at what age you could start using these active parenting skills? I responded with the story of the rocking chair. One day when our daughter, Megan, was only twelve months old she stood up in her rocking chair. I looked at her and said, "Megan, rocking chairs are for sitting. Please sit down." And she looked at me with that look that says, "And what are you going to do about it if I don't?"

Each one of us wants to influence our environment and gain some measure of control. We would like for things to go our way, and we want the *power* to make that happen. As parents, we want to empower our children to develop their talents and skills and become competent individuals who contribute to the common good. However, power is a double-edged sword. It can be used for better or for worse. Every parent knows the feeling of frustration that ensues when a child first learns to use her power to defy our authority. "What ARE we going to do about it if…?"

For the record, in my power struggle with Megan, I used a logical consequence and said, "Megan, either sit in the rocking chair or I'll have to take it away for the rest of the day." She stood there and looked at me. I calmly picked her up and put her aside, then took the chair out of the room. The next day when she stood in the rocking chair I again gave her the choice, "You can either sit in the rocking chair or I'll have to take it away again." Megan sat down, having learned the lesson in one take.

Rebellion and Power Struggles

When a child becomes discouraged trying to find power in positive ways he may turn to the easier approach of rebellion. The child can do this by trying to boss others around or by showing others that he can't be bossed. After all, the power to say, "no" is very powerful as every two-year-old knows. In fact, one of the basic rules of power is this:

The person in position to say "no" is in the more powerful position.

This is why power struggles are so frustrating for parents. We are bigger, smarter, more experienced and have the authority to decide what's in the best interest of our families—but even so, we cannot make our children do what we want. They have the free will to choose, and if they choose to resist us, our frustration can easily turn to anger. This feeling of anger is the major clue that you are in a power struggle and that your child has chosen a rebellious approach to his goal of power. The other clue is that power-driven children are very persistent and often respond to correction by continuing the misbehavior, often in open defiance. For example: "No! You can't make me!"

How parents pay off the negative approach of rebellion. The first step in avoiding or getting out of a power struggle is to recognize that our own behavior is often the "pay off" that keeps our child rebelling! Parents who tend towards the dictator style often fight fire with fire. Words such as, "No, you can't make me!" are fighting words to an autocratic parent. It hooks their own desire for power by triggering thoughts such as, "I've got to be in control here; I'm the parent!" and of course, "Oh yes I can!" They meet the child's challenge with a show of force and wind up fighting, either verbally or with punishment. Ironically, the more you fight with a child over power, the more she perceives that she is winning. After all, even if she eventually does what you want, say after a spanking or other punishment, she still has the secondary payoff of knowing that she made you angry. This in itself is very powerful and acts to reinforce the child's rebellious behavior. "Look how powerful I am. I made Daddy so mad!"

Parents who tend towards the doormat style often make the mistake of giving in to rebellious children. These parents want to avoid confrontation and give in to the child's unreasonable demands and refusals. The pay-off is that the child gets her own way. "Look how powerful I am. I made Daddy give in!"

Avoiding Power Struggles

The secret to avoiding a power struggle is to neither fight nor give in.

Remember, as soon as you get angry, you lose the power struggle.

This is not an easy task, but with a little parent "judo" it can be accomplished. While autocratic parents tend to fight head on with a challenging child, Judo is the art of sidestepping the opponent's attack, and using his own thrust to throw him off balance. By doing the unexpected and not fighting, yet not giving in, a parent can influence the child to change some of the thinking that drives the child's behavior. This requires first that we stay calm and do not take rebellion personally. (See the section on "managing anger" that follows.) Remember, as soon as you get angry, you lose the power struggle.

We can also "do the unexpected" and communicate more confidence in the child's ability to make decisions by himself. Rather than boss, we can give choices. We can let the child make some mistakes, and then experience the consequences...without lecturing or humiliating. We can set up family meetings to involve the child in making decisions that affect the whole family. We can use the Family Enrichment Activities, communication skills, and methods of encouragement described in this chapter to begin winning a more cooperative relationship. And, most important, we can show the child that we are not interested in fighting. Instead, we will work together to find solutions, and when discipline is necessary, we will use logical consequences and other respectful methods rather than anger and punishment.

The parent who tends toward the doormat style, in addition to using the Active Parenting skills just described, can refuse to give in to the child's unreasonable demands. We can stop being short-order cooks, clean-up services, wake-up callers, and last-minute chauffeurs. We can set firm limits, negotiate within those limits, refuse to be intimidated by displays of anger, and enforce the consequences of breaking the limits. We can let our children know that while we believe they should be treated respectfully, we expect to be treated respectfully as well. All of these ideas require that we assert some of our own power and recognize our responsibility to be the leader in the family.

Let's see how a number of Active Parenting skills can be combined to reduce the "flack" experienced in a power struggle.

The FLAC Method

The acronym, FLAC, can help you remember how to defuse a power struggle without fighting or giving in. The letters stand for:

Feelings

Limits

Alternatives

Consequences

Let's use the following situation as an example. Nine-year-old Justin is angry about going to bed and keeps getting up for one thing after another. His father is about to get very angry when he remembers that getting angry and shouting at Justin is what his son expects and will only fuel the power struggle between them. Instead, he does the unexpected and sits down on his son's bed and says:

Father: *I guess I really don't blame you for wanting to stay up later, Justin. I never liked going to bed, either. It feels like you're missing out on something, doesn't it?* **(F for Feelings)**

Justin: *(Surprised at his father's empathy) Yeah.*

Father: *Still, we all need our sleep to stay healthy and function well the next day, so you can't just stay up until you crash.* **(L for Limits)**

Justin: *But I don't want to go to bed now. It's too early.*

Father: *Hmm, well maybe there's an alternative. I might be willing to let you stay up an extra half hour if you were to use it as quiet time to relax yourself. Say, maybe by reading in bed.* **(A for Alternative)**

Justin: *Can I read fun stuff or does it have to be a schoolbook?*

Father: *You can read fun stuff. But here's the deal. If you are tired the next day or don't get up on time, or if you get out of bed after the half hour is up, then you have to go to bed on time the next night with no reading or hassle. Agreed?* **(C for Consequences)**

Justin: *Ok.*

Let's review the four steps:

Feelings. We saw in Chapter One how important it is to listen and respond to our children's feelings. When we show empathy for their feelings about the situation, we suddenly move from being the enemy to being on their side in finding a solution to a common problem. This goes a long way towards defusing the power struggle ("don't fight") while laying the groundwork for a win-win solution.

Limits. By reminding his son of the limits of the situation and providing a good reason for the limits, dad defines the problem to be solved ("don't give in"). It's much less provocative to say, "because the situation calls for this," rather than, "because I said so." In this case, the situation calls for a good night's sleep.

By negotiating within reasonable limits, we can often make the limits more palatable for our children.

Alternatives. Once people disengage from a struggle for power, you'd be surprised how often an acceptable alternative can be found. There is no magic number of minutes every child needs to sleep. The extra 30 minutes is unlikely to cause a problem, and it has the additional benefit of encouraging the importance of reading. By negotiating within reasonable limits, we can often make the limits more palatable for our children. Even when the limits are firm, you can often find an alternative within those limits that makes it more acceptable to the child.

Consequences. Some writers suggest that consequences only make matters worse with a rebellious child. Others suggest coming down even harder in a display of "tough love." However, if you can avoid getting angry (which turns the logical consequence into a punishment) then consequences can be useful as one more tool in motivating the child to live within the limits. They do not need to be harsh, just enough to remind the child that they are responsible for their actions.

Parenting and Anger

Children and adults who cannot control their temper create pain for themselves and those around them.

The management of anger has become recognized in recent years as vitally important to families and throughout society. Anger that turns to rage and then to violence creates headlines that range from school shootings and terrorist attacks to family violence. Even on smaller scales, children and adults who cannot control their temper create pain for themselves and those around them. Yet anger is also a natural part of life, so we are not quite sure what to make of this complicated emotion. Perhaps these pages will give you a new view of an old subject.

The Anatomy of Anger

Response to frustration. Anger is an emotional and physiological response to frustration. If an important need, want, or desire is blocked for us, our bodies and emotions react with intense feelings that we often label as anger.

For example, a caveman walking through the woods comes upon a fallen tree that blocks his path. On the other side of the tree are some berries he wants to pick and eat. He strains to push the fallen tree aside, but he isn't strong enough, and he becomes frustrated at the thought of not reaching his goal. His frustration produces physiological changes in his body that enable him to lift the fallen tree savagely and hurl it aside.

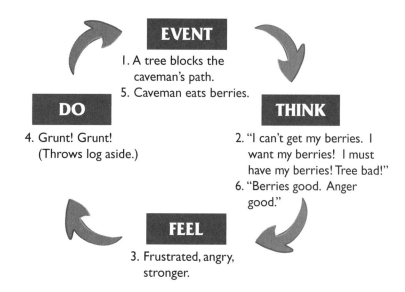

Purpose of anger. Anger releases certain chemicals into our bloodstream. These chemicals produce changes that make us stronger, faster, and look intimidating. This is known as the "fight/flight" syndrome, because it makes us ready to fight danger or run from it. In primitive times, the added power it produced helped us survive when problems were settled by brute force.

Old brain/new brain theory. Anger is associated with the so-called "old brain," which has been present in human beings since the beginning of our existence. But as the "new brain" has evolved around the old brain, so has human intelligence and societies based on law. This gives us the ability to handle problems with solutions other than brute force.

"Use," not "lose," our temper. However, even in modern societies, anger sometimes pays off. Rudolf Dreikurs once said that people do not "lose" their temper; they "use" their temper. What he meant was that people sometimes use anger to intimidate others into giving them what they want. Since anger is often accompanied by violence, this intimidation can sometimes be effective. But it carries a heavy price. Anger used to bully damages relationships and is hurtful. Worse yet, it can lead to violent behavior and crime.

How To Use Anger Positively

The Message of Anger

Our own angry feelings tell us that one of our goals is being blocked. It clearly sends this message:

> *"Act! Don't just sit there; get up and do something!"*

If we do something soon, we can often solve the problem before it gets worse, and before we "blow up." If we don't act but try to ignore the message, several things could happen:

1. The problem might go away by other means, but this is a risky and uncertain possibility.

2. Our anger may grow in intensity until it propels us into some action, which is likely to be desperate, unthinking, and potentially violent.

3. Our anger will seethe internally, expressing itself in unexpected ways: headaches, rashes, ulcers—even heart attacks.

How to Act on Anger

There are a number of useful ways to listen to the message of anger and take positive action:

1. Act to change the situation. (Do something different.) Struggle until you remove the fallen tree.

Example:

> *Use effective discipline skills such as "I" messages, logical consequences, and The FLAC method.*

2. Reduce the importance of the goal. Put it in perspective. Think something different.

Examples:

> *Although you may want the berries very much, be aware that you don't need them for your survival.*
>
> *Your child refuses to take a bath. Remind yourself that your goal of a daily bath is less important than your good relationship with your child and that missing a bath will not seriously affect your child.*

3. Change your goals. Find an alternative. Again, think something different.

Examples:

> *Decide that the berries are not the only solution to the hunger problem and look for an alternative—maybe an apple tree near the river.*
>
> *Give up your goal of having your child play the piano and encourage an alternative activity of her choice.*

Helping Children Use Their Anger

Teach children that violence is not an okay way to solve problems.

Because children are usually more primitive in their expression of emotions, they will often resemble the caveman when experiencing frustration and anger. Tantrums and hitting are fairly common with young children. However, it is increasingly important in these days of "zero tolerance" for aggressive behavior that we teach children that violence is not an okay way to solve problems. There are several ways parents can help:

1. Give them a good model. The way you handle your own problems and frustrations will provide a model for your children.

- *Do you fly into a rage, hurling insults and humiliating remarks?*
- *Do you strike out at others?*
- *Do you sink into a depression (an adult temper tantrum or "silent storm")?*

2. Guide them with words to find more effective forms of expression.

Examples:

"You have the right to feel the way you do, but in our family, we don't scream and blame; we look for solutions."

"I can see that you are angry. Can you tell me with words instead of hitting?"

"When you get angry at me, please tell me without calling me names. I don't call you names; please don't call me names."

"Take your sails out of their wind."

3. Remove yourself from a power struggle. When children have tantrums, you can acknowledge their anger, but at the same time "take your sails out of their wind." Don't try to overpower the child; withdraw instead. This action says to the child, "I am not intimidated by your show of temper and will not give in, but I won't punish or humiliate you either." The result is that children who get neither a fight nor their own way after throwing tantrums will usually find more acceptable ways to influence people. If you need a quiet place to withdraw from the power struggle, try the bathroom. It's the one place where a little privacy is usually expected.

4. Use the FLAC Method. In those situations where a child's tantrum interferes with the rights of others (like in a restaurant, or when company is in the home), you can acknowledge the child's feeling, remind him of the limits, offer an alternative, and follow through with logical consequences.

For example:

> *I know you are angry about having to go shopping with me, and I'll admit that it isn't much fun. Still, we do want to eat dinner tonight so we need to get this done. How about if you help me out by putting the food in the cart? That will make it go faster and then you can help me pick out some of your favorite desserts.*

If the child continues to act out his anger, add a logical consequence:

> *Dennis, you can either calm down and help me shop or we will have to go sit in the car until you can, then we definitely won't have time to stop by the park.*

Children must learn that there are consequences for violent and aggressive behavior.

Children must learn that there are consequences for violent and aggressive behavior. The child who acts out his anger by breaking something can help pay for its replacement. The child who hits or bullies can be removed from other kids for a period of time to think about how he can make it up to the other person. As with all logical consequences, stay calm and firm when delivering them. Your goal is not to hurt the child, which may just begin a revenge cycle, but rather to teach him.

5. Allow your child to influence your decisions. When a person feels powerless to influence leaders, frustration gives way to anger and rebellion. If you allow your child to influence your decisions concerning her, she will not be as likely to resort to such unconscious tactics as bedwetting, soiling, and stomach disorders, to name a few.

The method your child uses to influence your decisions will be influenced by what you allow to work. If you "give in" to tantrums, whining, or tears, the child will learn to use these tactics again. If you redirect your child to express his anger respectfully, listen to his arguments, and sometimes change your decisions, then your child learns the important skill of negotiation.

Courage ... One From the Heart

If parents and children both need power to survive and thrive, they need a character filled with courage even more. In fact, preparing a child to courageously meet the challenges life will certainly offer is perhaps the single most important aspect of parenting. Courage is such an important quality in today's complex world of choices that it forms the very foundation upon which the child constructs her personality. In fact, psychologist Alfred Adler and world leader Winston Churchill both said that it is the most important of all traits because it is the one on which all others depend. From the French word coeur, meaning "heart," courage is the "heart" that enables us to take risks. And it is through risk-taking that we are able to develop responsibility, cooperation, independence ... and whatever else we may strive for. In fact, we define courage in Active Parenting Now as:

The confidence to take a known risk for a known purpose.

Courage is a feeling. It is a feeling of confidence that motivates us to take risks, knowing that we have a chance to succeed, and that even if we fail, the risk was worth taking. Courage is not the absence of fear but the willingness to take a reasonable risk in spite of fear. Without this feeling of courage, we often find ourselves sitting on the sidelines, unwilling to take the risks inherent in any endeavor. Without courage, we let life pass us by while we wishfully wait for someone else to do it for us.

Courage and Fear

Courage first met fear
When I was still a child;
Courage gazed with cool, clear eyes;
Fear was something wild.

Courage urged, "Let's go ahead."
Fear said, "Let's turn back."
Courage spoke of what we had;
Fear of what we lacked.

Courage took me by the hand
And warmed my frozen bone;
Yet Fear the while tugged at my legs
And whispered, "We're alone."

Many have been the obstacles
Since first I had to choose,
And sometimes when Courage led me on
I've come up with a bruise.

And many have been the challenges
Since Fear and Courage met,
And yet those times I've followed Fear,
Too often—tagged along Regret.

Michael H. Popkin

Self-Esteem ... One From the Mind

Where does courage come from? It comes from a belief in ourselves that we are lovable, capable human beings who will eventually succeed. And even if we fail, we are still lovable, capable human beings. This belief in ourselves is commonly called "self-esteem." In other words we hold ourselves in high regard. When we think well of ourselves, when we think we have a good chance to succeed, then it makes sense that we will have the courage to take risks.

High Self-Esteem ➡ COURAGE

This courage usually produces more positive behaviors, including the perseverance to keep trying when the going gets tough. The result is often success and positive feedback from others, which strengthens self-esteem and courage in a success cycle.

SUCCESS CYCLE

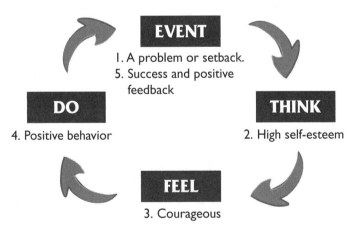

EVENT
1. A problem or setback.
5. Success and positive feedback

DO
4. Positive behavior

THINK
2. High self-esteem

FEEL
3. Courageous

As we can see in the graphic, a success cycle doesn't mean that our children will never run into problems or failure, but rather, that they will be able to handle these problems effectively and eventually succeed. The opposite of a success cycle might be called a failure cycle. When self-esteem is low, kids often lack the courage to take positive risks and either fail to try at all, or turn to easier misbehavior to reach their goals. Such behavior often produces failure and negative feedback from others, which lowers self-esteem further and produces more discouragement in a downward spiral of failure.

FAILURE CYCLE

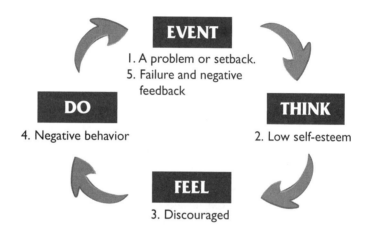

EVENT
1. A problem or setback.
5. Failure and negative feedback

THINK
2. Low self-esteem

FEEL
3. Discouraged

DO
4. Negative behavior

What Can Parents Do?

Helping our children get into success cycles and stay there is a goal for all parents. Helping our children develop the character to be successful within the rules and limits of society is a responsibility of all parents. It is therefore important for us to become skilled at encouraging the development of self-esteem, courage, and other qualities of good character. But what does that word "encouraging" really mean?

"En-courage" means to "instill courage." Rudolf Dreikurs once said "children need encouragement like plants need water."

Breaking the word into two parts, "en-courage" means to "instill courage." Rudolf Dreikurs once said "children need encouragement like plants need water." Encouragement is the fertilizer that nourishes our children's courage, self-esteem, character, and skills. Wherever it is applied, we see more growth in that area. Do you want your child to be a good reader? Encourage her reading. Do you want him to be honest? Encourage acts of honesty. What about responsibility, cooperation, and courage? Again, where you sprinkle encouragement you spur growth. The remainder of this chapter will help you strengthen your skills in this critical area of parenting.

Encouragement: "Catch 'em Doing Good"

Imagine yourself in this situation:

> *You are driving home in your car. Suddenly, in your rearview mirror you see a police car with blue lights flashing, and it is following you. Anxiously, you pull over, wondering what you did wrong. You notice your rapid heartbeat, the perspiration forming on your palms, your dry mouth. The policeman approaches your car window and asks for your driver's license. He looks at the license, then at you, and says, "You know, I've been on the force for 12 years, and it's always a pleasure to see a courteous driver. I pulled you over so I could congratulate you on the fine driving skill you showed back there in that traffic tangle at the freeway overpass. If every driver were as courteous and considerate as you, we could avoid lots of snarls and headaches. So I just wanted to say, 'Thanks.'"*

What do you think your reactions would be to the policeman's comment?

    a.   You would feel good about yourself; you'd be a little proud.

    b.   You would feel that you are a pretty good driver.

    c.   You would feel encouraged to drive more courteously and considerately in the future.

    d.   You'd almost faint from the shock!

The chances are response "d" was your strongest. We just do not expect to receive such compliments from authority figures. And yet, in the above example, after the shock has worn off and you are driving away, you probably would feel good about yourself, think that you are a pretty good driver, and feel encouraged to drive more courteously and considerately in the future.

Because most of us are not natural-born encouragers, we need to work at recognizing our own discouraging tendencies while strengthening our ability to encourage.

The policeman's comment was an example of the power of encouragement. With only a few words, he increased your self-esteem, gave a boost to your confidence, and created the likelihood that you would drive even better in the future. No wonder some call encouragement "the subtle giant."

The down side of encouragement is that in every opportunity to encourage our children (as well as ourselves and others) there is also an opportunity to discourage them or "remove courage." Because most of us are not natural-born encouragers, we need to work at recognizing our own discouraging tendencies while strengthening our ability to encourage. Before we look further at encouragement, let's consider its opposite—discouragement—and the ways it affects children's behavior.

Avoid Discouraging

The misbehaving child is usually a discouraged child.

The misbehaving child is usually a discouraged child. Somewhere along the line, he has lost the courage to face life's problems with positive behavior. Such children have come to believe that the only path open to them is the easier, negative approach to their goals.

In order to build children's self-esteem, and courage, we want to first become aware of some common ways we may be discouraging them. Referring again to the think-feel-do cycle, if we become discouraging events in our children's lives, we tend to lower their self-esteem, which leads to discouragement, which leads to negative behavior ... which may prompt us to become even more punishing and discouraging. To change this cycle, we want to do our best to become encouraging events in our children's think-feel-do cycle. Although abuse and neglect are the most serious forms of discouragement, we are going to focus our attention on four less obvious ways that parents sometimes discourage their children and how these can be turned into methods of encouragement.

DISCOURAGING EVENTS	ENCOURAGING EVENTS
Overprotection and pampering	Stimulating Independence
Focusing on mistakes	Building on strengths
Expecting too little	Showing Confidence
Expecting too much (perfectionism)	Valuing the child as is

Overprotection vs. Stimulating Independence

If somebody who is important to you spends too much time telling you how dangerous and difficult the world is, you may come to believe that you can't handle things for yourself. You may let him handle problems for you, depriving you of a chance to learn from the experience. If you get in trouble at school or with the law, he is there to bail you out. And if you never experience the consequences of your mistakes, you begin to get the idea that you can do anything you like. But strangely you find yourself not feeling very confident, though you may act over-confident to make up for it.

If you find that your parents are constantly waiting on you, picking up after you, reminding you of things and otherwise pampering you, you come to expect that treatment from others. When they do not treat you the same, you find that things start falling through the cracks and mistakes multiply. You become angry and blame others, then wonder why your relationships are not satisfying. Statements like the following may be well intentioned, but they are counterproductive:

> *"Sure, I'll be glad to go down to the school and talk to your teacher. I'm sure when she realizes how hard you worked, she'll change your grade."*

> *"I shouldn't have to call you three times to get up in the morning, but at least you're getting to school on time.*

How to stimulate independence

Haim Ginott wrote, "Dependence breeds hostility."

Independence, or the ability to stand on one's own two feet, is essential for thriving in our modern society. In fact, when we keep our children overly dependent on us, not only do they pay a price, but so do we. As psychologist Haim Ginott wrote, "Dependence breeds hostility." Overprotecting and pampering do not lead to the appreciation that many parents expect. It leads to resentment! The last thing we want to do as parents is to keep our children overly dependent on us. Our job as parents is to work ourselves out of a job.

Our job as parents is to work ourselves out of a job.

As we encourage our children toward independence, we also want to keep in mind that they will benefit enormously by learning to cooperate, as we mentioned in Chapter One. The phrase, "no man is an island," expresses the truth that interdependence—independent individuals choosing to work together cooperatively—offers the best chance for success of both the individual and the human community.

Avoid pampering your child. When parents put themselves into the child's service or otherwise treat the child like a privileged character, the child eventually becomes dependent, spoiled, and discouraged. Some signs of pampering a child include: calling her more than once to get up in the morning; routinely driving her places on short notice; picking out her clothes; giving her money on demand instead of an allowance; allowing her to curse at you or otherwise speak disrespectfully; not monitoring media such as TV, music, movies, and the internet; making her homework your responsibility; allowing her to frequently eat meals in front of the TV; always cleaning up after her; not requiring her to help with family chores; and rescuing her from the consequences of her misbehavior.

If you find some of these examples hitting home, then you can let your child know that you have decided to stop pampering her, and begin treating her more respectfully. You can do this in a firm yet friendly way, taking responsibility yourself, while even encouraging the child. For example:

Let your child know that you have decided to stop pampering her, and begin treating her more respectfully.

"I want to apologize for treating you like you didn't have the good sense to handle _____ (e.g., getting yourself up in the morning; your own money; your own homework; picking up your own clothes). From now on I'm going to stop treating you like a baby and leave it up to you."

"I don't use that kind of language when I'm angry with you; I don't expect you to use it when you are angry with me."

"I'll be glad to show you where dirty clothes go, but from now on I'm only washing the clothes that get put there."

Help the child develop a sense of interdependence.   Life in our diverse, modern society is neither independent nor dependent. It is interdependent. We are all traveling in the same boat, and learning to work cooperatively with others is a key to individual success as well as the common welfare. You can invite cooperative behavior on the part of your child, with the aim of letting him experience the pleasure and benefits of group efforts.

"You're an important part of this family, and we'd like your ideas at family meetings."

"Why don't you come up on the sofa and snuggle with us?"

"Would you like to make lasagna with us?"

Allow natural consequences to teach.   Children learn an amazing amount of valuable life lessons from direct experience of the consequences afforded by Mother Nature. This method of learning is so effective that it deserves a name: natural consequences.

Natural consequences are the results that naturally occur as a result of a child's behavior without the parent doing anything.

Here are some examples:

The natural consequence of not eating breakfast is getting hungry before lunch.

The natural consequence of oversleeping on a school day is being late for school.

The natural consequence of leaving your bicycle outside may be that it gets rusty or that it is stolen.

Natural consequences are particularly effective for teaching independence because the parent can be a sympathetic third party, rather than the disciplinarian. Of course, to be effective we have to avoid two temptations: 1) to rescue (for example, buy him a new bike); and 2) to say "I told you so." (How much better to say, "Gee, I know that's frustrating," rather than "I told you this would happen if you didn't put that bike away!")

When Natural Consequences Cannot Be Used as Teachers

There are many situations when our best course of action is to stay out of the way and let the natural consequences teach the lesson. However, there are three circumstances in which a responsible parent cannot simply allow Mother Nature to take her toll:

There are many situations when our best course of action is to stay out of the way and let the natural consequences teach the lesson.

1. **When the natural consequences may be catastrophic.** For example, the natural consequences of running into a busy street may be death.

2. **When the natural consequences are so far into the future that the child is not concerned about the connection.** For example, the natural consequences of not brushing her teeth may lead to eventual tooth decay.

3. **When the natural consequences of a child's behavior affect others rather than the child.** For example, the child borrows your scissors and loses them.

In these situations the parent owns the problem, and it is up to the parent to use the discipline skills covered in Chapters Two and Three to take action to prevent such natural consequences from occurring or reoccurring.

Building on Strengths vs. Focusing on Mistakes

If somebody who is important to you spends a lot of time telling you what you do wrong, you come to believe there is more wrong with you than right. If that important person yells or sounds disgusted with you, it hurts even more. If he calls you names or attacks your character, you may begin to believe that you are as bad as he says that you are. Ironically, it becomes harder to do things right because you are so worried about making mistakes and creating further disappointment.

Maybe you have worked hard to correct a problem or improve your behavior and all she notices is what is still not right. You feel that your effort has not been appreciated, and wonder why you should bother to try again in the future. You lose motivation and your performance drops further, which prompts more discouraging comments until finally you feel like a certified loser.

> *"I notice you left your glass in the den again last night. How many times do I have to ask you to be more considerate?"*
>
> *"This doesn't look good where you colored outside the lines, does it?"*
>
> *"Did you notice how your man beat you down court for that easy basket? You've really got to hustle back on defense."*

Building on Strengths: The BANK Method

Kids do need to know what mistakes they have made in order to learn from the experience and do better in the future. We are not suggesting that you never mention a mistake or misbehavior. The mistake most parents make is to point out the mistakes and misbehavior, but then ignore the successes and

If you and your child are locked in a power struggle or revenge cycle and want to break out, find something about the child that you like.

positive behavior. The key to building successful behavior, however, is to focus the majority of your feedback on what your kids are doing right. This builds their confidence and motivates them to want to keep improving. In fact, if you and your child are locked in a power struggle or revenge cycle and want to break out, find something about the child that you like. Focusing your attention on what's right with your children, rather than what is wrong, is tremendously encouraging. And, as we've seen, encouragement leads to improved self-esteem, which leads to courage and positive behavior ... in other words, a success cycle.

The BANK Method of Encouragement

B aby Steps

A cknowledge

N udge

K eep encouraging!

To help you remember how to use this important aspect of encouragement effectively keep in mind these four letters: B-A-N-K. Just as a bank is a place where resources are invested for growth, you can use the BANK method to help your child build her personal assets and grow into a successful human being. Let's look at the four letters one by one:

B for Baby steps. The key to building on strengths is to break the learning down into baby steps. Remember, you didn't learn to walk all at once. You learned step by step. This learning process is the same for most things. Whether it is helping a child learn to complete his homework, or teaching him to be honest, we can systematically build on strengths to help our children build skills, values, and character.

"I know school can be difficult, but if we break each assignment down into small steps you'll find that you can do it."

"If we want to teach Dani to be honest, I think we need to take it day by day and encourage her every time she tells the truth when she could have lied or deceived us."

It is much more effective to "catch 'em doing good" than our traditional approach of catching them doing bad.

A for Acknowledge what your child does well. Once you have identified a goal for your child (for example, having good study habits or being an honest individual), get an idea where the child is on the path towards reaching that goal. It is unlikely that he can't read a single word or answers every question with a lie—so he will be somewhere in between. Now you have a place to start. Acknowledge what he can already do well in order to build confidence and motivation to take the next step.

"This is terrific! You've completed two assignments. This is the way to get ahead at school. I can really see that you've worked hard at this, but then I know you can work hard . . . I've seen you on the basketball court."

"I'm not thrilled that you borrowed my hammer without asking, but I do appreciate your owning up to it when I asked. I appreciate your honesty."

It is much more effective to "catch 'em doing good" than our traditional approach of catching them doing bad. In addition to acknowledging their progress, it also helps to acknowledge other areas where the child is already experiencing some success. This helps build the self-esteem that translates into risk taking and other successes. The parent who brought in the basketball connection in the previous example was using this strength-building technique effectively.

Examples like the following offer children a healthy diet of encouragement:

"It was really a pleasure having you out to dinner with us tonight. Your manners were great. Let's do it again soon."

"Thank you for helping with the dishes."

"I appreciate your playing quietly while I took a nap. That was very considerate."

"It sure is fun to play with you when you take turns with me."

N for Nudge the child to take the next step. Children get a sense of self-esteem from learning, whether they are learning a sport, a school subject, or a skill. As we have seen, learning requires many steps and gradual improvement. It also requires risk, because with each new step, there is the potential for failure. Even with children who have strong self-esteem, there are times when fear of failure paralyzes them, making it difficult to take the next step. And there are times for all of us when the frustration of not progressing the way we'd like undermines our courage to persevere and tempts us to give up. This is when an encouraging nudge from a parent or teacher can help give the child enough courage to take the next baby step. For example:

"Learning to do division can be frustrating, and I guess you feel like giving up. But if you'll just stick with it, I know you'll get it. Look how far you've come already! Now, how about tackling that last problem again?"

"I know it hasn't been easy, but you've really improved in being honest with us. And we're feeling like we can trust you more. So, if you still want to spend the night at Carrie's house, it's okay with us."

"You can do it. Go ahead."

"Keep trying. You'll get it."

"Let's take a break then try again."

"Sometimes a rest can help. Let's try again tomorrow."

K for Keep encouraging improvement and effort. Arthur Blank, co-founder of the tremendously successful Home Depot and owner of the Atlanta Falcons pro football team once said that although he is a highly competitive person, he never sees the finish line. In other words, life is a process where success is measured in growth and improvement rather than any single end result. The mistake most people make in the encouragement process is to wait until the child attains a desired goal before offering encouragement. One misguided father actually said that he was waiting for his son to graduate before complimenting him on his school work!

Any improvement, no matter how small, is a step in the right direction and should be noticed and acknowledged.

Since a key to encouragement is to break the process down into baby steps, it is important to offer encouragement along the entire route. Any improvement, no matter how small, is a step in the right direction and should be noticed and acknowledged. Since success is a great motivator, we want the child to be able to experience numerous successes along the way. This builds self-esteem and keeps the child moving towards the goal. If the child falls back a step (and that's to be expected) she needs our encouragement to keep at it and not give up. In fact, her effort alone, even when she's not making progress, should always be encouraged.

> *"Great! You are really getting good at writing down all of your assignments. One more day and you'll have a whole week."*

> *"Thanks for telling us about not turning in your homework on Monday. That took a lot of courage. We'll talk about what to do about it in a minute, but first I want you to know how much we admire your efforts to be more honest."*

> *"I can really see the effort that went into this."*

> *"Hey, this room is really looking good. You've gotten all your books picked up, and the bed's made. If you like, I have some time and could help you figure out a system for organizing your closet."*

> *"I really like the way you stick with it."*

Showing Confidence vs. Expecting too Little

If people who are important to you don't believe in your ability, you probably won't believe in it either. They don't have to say so; you can usually tell what they think of you by the way they act around you and the words they use with you. You pick up on those things pretty easily. If they never ask your opinion you guess that they don't think you have much useful to say. If they seem satisfied with half-hearted efforts at school, you figure they think that mediocrity is all you are capable of. If they do not encourage you to participate in a sport or other activity, you can sense that they don't think you can handle it. Of course, sometimes they make their opinions of you crystal clear by saying such things as:

"No, you can't use that! You'll break it."

"I guess you're just not the type who does well in school."

How To Show Confidence

When those we value most show confidence in our abilities we tend to gain confidence in ourselves.

A cornerstone of self-esteem and courage is the belief that we are capable of success, whether it is in school, at work, with friends, family, or a love relationship. As we achieve success in solving life's problems and learning new skills, our belief in ourselves grows. But tackling problems and attempting new skills takes confidence. When those we value most show confidence in our abilities we tend to gain confidence in ourselves.

There was a famous experiment in which teachers were told that results from an intelligence test showed that some of the students in their classes were highly intelligent and capable of excellent work while others were not. What the teachers did not know was that the results of the intelligence test had nothing to do with which students they were told were brighter. In fact, the students had been assigned at random. At the end of the year the students' grades were compared. Guess which group did better? As you might expect, the students in the so-called "intelligent" group had higher grades. The teacher's expectation that they were capable had made a significant difference in the students' ability to succeed. Such is the power of positive expectations on performance.

Parents can also help their children succeed by showing confidence in them. Here are some ways to do this:

Give responsibilities in line with what you know about your child's abilities.

Give responsibility. Giving your child responsibility is a nonverbal way of showing confidence. It is a way of saying, "I know you can do this." Of course, you want to give responsibilities in line with what you know about your child's abilities, or the standards may be set too high. Here are some examples of giving responsibility in ways that demonstrate confidence:

> *"I will agree to your keeping the dog, Julie, if you will accept the responsibility of feeding and caring for her."*
>
> *"I think you have handled getting yourself up in the morning really well, so you can probably handle staying up later now—say, 9:00 p.m. What do you think?"*

When you ask your child's opinion, you are demonstrating confidence in his ability to make a useful contribution.

Ask your child's opinion or advice. Children like to have parents lean on their knowledge or judgment. When you ask your child's opinion, you are demonstrating confidence in his ability to make a useful contribution. If you ask your child to teach you something, it shows confidence in his knowledge and skills. Asking for his opinions in such ways helps bolster his self-esteem:

> *"Which route do you think would be best on our trip to visit Grandma and Grandpa?"*
>
> *"What would you like to do with the toys that get left on the floor?"*
>
> *"Would you teach me how to play the new video game?"*
>
> *"Well, what were the reasons for the Civil War?"*

Avoid the temptation to take over. It is an act of confidence in our children's abilities when we refuse to step in and take over when they become discouraged. What a temptation it is, this tendency to relieve their discomfort by doing the thing that is so hard for them and so easy for us! But when we give in to the temptation, we are not showing confidence in the child. If we do something for the child on a regular basis that she, with a little persistence, could do independently, then we are communicating a lack of confidence in her ability to follow a task through to the end. When we bail her out of the consequences of misbehavior, we rob her of an important lesson in responsibility. We say in effect that we don't have confidence in her ability to handle the consequences of her actions.

All in all, taking over is not a way to encourage children who are discouraged; it is a way to certify their discouragement. Such children often show an inability to tolerate frustration. When things don't work out immediately, they give up—often having a "frustration tantrum" in which they are overwhelmed with anger and frustration at their inability to accomplish a task. Instead, encourage your child to stick with it with words such as these:

> *"Keep trying, you can do it!"*
> *"No, I can't stop the kids from teasing you, but I can talk to you about some things that you can do."*

Expect success and positive behavior. Like the teachers in the study who expected certain students to succeed, your expectations of your children are powerful influencers of their behavior. In fact,

Children often live up or down to our expectations.

Your expectations of your children are powerful influencers of their behavior.

So, why not expect them to succeed? When you let them know that you think they can do it—whether "it" is doing well in school, being polite in social situations, following family rules and values, or anything else—you are encouraging them to live up to your expectations. They will sometimes mess up, and they will need your encouragement not to give up when this happens. And of course, you want to keep your expectations in line with reality. After all, expecting a child to go from Cs and Ds to straight As overnight is setting you both up for failure. But expecting that your child can improve and using the BANK method to encourage his improvement is a recipe for success.

"I know you can improve your grades if you set your mind on it."

"I'm counting on you to use your best manners when we are at Grandma's."

"I expect you to tell me the truth."

"Just keep practicing and you'll get it."

Valuing the Child vs. Expecting Too Much (Perfectionism)

Positive expectations are important. However, if your parents expect more from you than you are able to give, you gradually stop trying because you know you will never be able to satisfy them. You may decide to make your

mark in other ways, like misbehaving. Since you can't be the best at being the best, maybe you will set your goal at being the best at being the worst. Or maybe you will decide to become a perfectionist yourself in a futile attempt to please your parents and yourself. Life becomes one big worry as you try harder and harder to succeed. But even when you do succeed, you cannot enjoy your success for fear of what challenge to your self-esteem is coming next.

"How did you misspell 'circus' when you got all the others right? If you'd really thought about it, you would have had a perfect paper."

"This isn't a bad report card. But with your potential, you could have done better."

"You've got to practice, practice, practice if you ever want to be a really good violinist."

How To Value the Child

A child's self-esteem does not spring from achievements alone. Much more important for most people is that they are accepted by significant people in their lives—that they belong. In fact, much of our effort to be successful is really fueled by our desire to win the acceptance of those significant people. Ironically, what most of us really want deep down inside is to be accepted for just being ourselves, not just for our achievements. This is what it means to feel a sense of belonging.

Children who feel accepted by their parents have a tremendous bedrock of self-esteem upon which to construct a healthy, happy life.

The baseball pitcher, Tim Wakefield, was once asked before pitching the biggest game of his young career if he was nervous. His answer was no, because, he reasoned, no matter what happened that night, the next day three things would still be true: his parents would still love him, his friends would still love him, and God would still love him. Armed with that core sense of self-esteem and acceptance for who he was, his success in life, as measured by personal satisfaction, was well on its way.

Children who feel accepted by their parents have a tremendous bedrock of self-esteem upon which to construct a healthy, happy life. Without it, some of the richest, most successful people in history have lived lives of quiet desperation, wondering why their successes were never satisfying.

The goal is to communicate to our children that win or lose, pass or fail, in the limelight or in the line-up, we are still their parents and we are glad of it. We all need this unconditional acceptance from someone, and if we don't get it from our parents, we need to get it someplace else: from a substitute parent, or even a therapist. For some, a belief in God fulfills this same human need for unconditional acceptance.

Separate worth from accomplishments. A child's worth is less a matter of what he does, and more a matter of who he is. You can let your child know that while you admire his successes and share disappointment in his failures, you love him for himself. You can put emphasis on the importance of participation in the activities themselves and not just on the results. You can encourage your child while he is doing a task instead of waiting until the task is completed.

> *"I'm glad you enjoy learning."*
> *"Playing your hardest is more important than winning."*
> *"Losing doesn't make a person a loser."*

There are no bad children, only bad behavior.   Help them accept mistakes with a smile rather than a kick.

There are no bad children, only bad behavior.

Separate worth from misbehavior. Just as a child's worth is something different from the sum total of her accomplishments, it is also different from her misbehaviors. A useful way to approach this is with the attitude that there are no bad children, only bad behavior. If a child is labeled "bad" or "no good" he may eventually come to believe that the label is true. When this happens, bad behavior then becomes appropriate. After all, what should we expect from "bad" people but "bad" behavior? This self-fulfilling prophecy makes it vitally important that we refrain from labeling or shaming children for their mistakes or misbehavior. Children who grow up ashamed of themselves have a difficult time regaining their lost self-esteem and courage.

Mistakes, like misbehavior, are not indications of a lack of worth, but are actually part of growth and development. A mistake can teach a valuable lesson, showing a child what not to do in the future. We want to help children, especially perfectionists, learn to make friends with their mistakes. Mistakes, as we have said, are tools for learning, not crimes to be ashamed of.

Children (and adults) who are afraid of being imperfect actually retard their own growth and development. A perfectionist, according to one joke, is a person who won't attempt a foreign language until he can speak it fluently. As this quip implies, a fear of mistakes yields a fear of trying, which in turn

Help them accept mistakes with a smile rather than a kick.

yields less learning. Since one of our goals is to help children learn, we want to help them accept mistakes with a smile rather than a kick.

> *"No, you're not bad, but coloring on the walls is a bad thing to do. Let's find a good place to color."*
>
> *"When we get angry at you, it doesn't mean we don't like you. It means we don't like something you've done."*
>
> *"Mistakes are for learning. When we make a mistake, we don't blame. We correct it."*
>
> *"I guess you made a mistake. Well, let's see what you can learn from it."*

Independence, or the ability to stand on one's own two feet, is essential for thriving in our democratic society.

You can say and do things that show your child you love her for her unique self, and for no other reason.

Appreciate the child's uniqueness. Although it is important to teach children that all people are equal, that doesn't mean all people are the same. It is encouraging for your child to know that she is unique, special, one of a kind. You can appreciate your child's uniqueness by taking an interest in her activities. Most of all, you can say and do things that show your child you love her for her unique self, and for no other reason.

> *"Anyway, that's my opinion. What's yours?"*
>
> *"When I see you from a distance, I can tell it's you from your walk."*
>
> *"This room is really you! I could never have decorated it for you."*
>
> *"You are the only you in the whole world. What luck that you happen to be my daughter!"*
>
> *"I love you."*

Family Enrichment Activity: Letter of Encouragement

As a young Sunday School teacher, I became annoyed with the idea of having to give grades to my students. Grades seemed an inadequate way to express either their progress or the way I felt about them after sharing nine months together. I decided to write each of my students a personal letter to go with the grades. While writing the letters, I found myself describing the positive aspects of each child and how he or she was progressing. These "letters of encouragement" were received appreciatively as the children left for summer vacation.

I didn't think much more about the letters until four years later. I was at a reception when a woman approached me and introduced herself as the mother of one of my students from that same Sunday School class. "That letter you wrote Alice meant so much to her," she said. "You know she still has it on her bulletin board."

All of the encouragement skills discussed in this session could be considered as family enrichment activities. But somehow "putting it in writing" carries that extra weight that makes it special. In addition, the child can refer back to a letter of encouragement in the future and rekindle the warm feeling it generated, just as Alice did. This week's activity is to write a letter of encouragement to each of your children. Let your letter have the following characteristics:

- Write about your child's improvement in some area, not necessarily per-fection.

- Write only truthful statements; don't say that the child has improved when he really hasn't.

- Be specific about what the improvements are.

- Write how the child's behavior has been helpful to others.

A sample letter might look like this:

Dear Ben,

Your mother and I have been noticing how well you are doing with your reading. We can really hear the improvement. All your hard work is really paying off! Pretty soon you will be able to read anything you want to all by yourself. You can't imagine how wonderful a thing that is, and we are so happy for you.

I am also proud of the way you are accepting responsibility for your schoolwork. You are taking time to do your homework every school night like we talked about. You are also giving it your best and not rushing to get it done. Your teacher seems to have noticed the improvement, also. That must make you feel good.

Thanks also for helping me clean up the garage the other day. You have grown to where you are a big help in getting things done. Plus, you have always been great company with your sense of humor and positive attitude. And if I forget to say it often enough, I'm real glad that you are my son.

Love,
Dad

Family Meeting: Emphasizing the Family Unit

Active Parenting believes that families are the backbone of civilization and that your family is the most important family in the world…to your children. History has proven time after time that alone we could never survive, but by forming small cooperative units we could thrive. Families have been a source of belonging, learning, and contributing for children and for society—and, to a large extent, the measure of any civilization rests on the strength of its families.

So whether you are part of a traditional Mom-and-Dad family, or whether it's a blended stepfamily, a single-parent family, or any other style of family—it's important for you to look for ways to let your children know that they are part of a family unit. Plan frequent family activities; use phrases like "in our family," and develop your own family traditions and rituals. And give your children the gift of memories by telling and retelling the special stories of your family's history—stories that make your family unique.

Take some time this week to gather the family together to talk about some aspect of your family history, such as how your family came to live in this country. Tell whatever special stories that you can remember that have been passed down, and answer their questions with encouragement. If you don't know much about your family history, consider making it a family project to find out. There is an abundance of family heritage information on the Internet, and your local library can help, too.

Remember also that through your family your children will learn that they belong to a much larger family, the family of humankind. And since their contributions to that family will help determine "the future of all people," your job as a parent may very well be the most important job in the world.

Chapter 3

HOME ACTIVITIES

- Practice "Stimulating Independence" and complete the guidesheet on page 138.

- Practice "Building on Strenths" and complete the guidesheet on page 139.

- Practice "Showing Confidence" and complete the guidesheet on page 140.

- Find ways to show that you value your child as he or she is, and complete the guidesheet on page 141.

- Write and give each of your children a letter of encouragement, and complete the guidesheet on page 142.

- Hold a family meeting to emphasize your family unity, and complete the guidesheet on page 143.

- Take a few moments to think about the things you've learned from this guide, and answer the questions found on page 144.

A child is a person who is going to carry on what you have started.

He is going to sit where you are sitting, and when you are gone,

Attend to those things which you think are important.

You may adopt all the policies you please, but how they are carried out depends on him.

He will assume control of your cities, states , and nations.

He is going to move in and take over your churches, schools, universities, and corporations.

All your books are going to be judged, praised, or condemned by him.

The fate of humanity is in his hands.

—Abraham Lincoln

The Job of My Life

Sometimes I wonder what to say
To make it better, to make it okay.
Sometimes I wonder just what to do,
Where to take a stand,
And how to help them through
Through the tough times and the glad times
The time we share as a family.
It's not long
The time we have together
Together as a family.
Active Parenting
The most important job in my life.
Active Parenting
Helped me do the job of my life.

And so I'm giving it all I can.
I'm a special part of a special plan.
And joy is growing within my heart
For my precious child as we make this start.
Active Parenting
The most important job in my life.
Active Parenting
Helped me do the job of my life.
Long ago, we didn't know
What challenges lay ahead
But now the joy is real,
And it's such a different feel
To love this child with my eyes opened wide.
Learning more each day
About the Active Parenting way
Active Parenting
The most important job in my life.
Active Parenting
Helped me do the job of my life.

—Michael H. Popkin

Use these worksheets to reinforce the skills taught in this guide.
See the Home Activities at the end of each chapter for
a schedule and instructions for use.

The Method of Choice Activity

Choices I can give my child this week:

_____

Child's name:

_____

Choice Given:

_____

How did it go?

_____

Child's name:

_____

Choice Given:

_____

How did it go?

_____

Child's name:

_____

Choice Given:

_____

How did it go?

_____

Child's name:

_____

Choice Given:

_____

How did it go?

_____

Who Owns the Problem Video Practice

Scene	Who Owns the Problem?	Why?
Katy and Ben (fighting)		
Sandra and Ramon (getting up)		
Sherry and Angela (interrupting)		
_____ _____ _____ (a problem in your family)		

This worksheet refers to the 3-week Active Parenting Now in 3 *discussion program. If you are using this Parent's Guide independently and are interested in participating in a discussion group, check out the Parent tab at our website for a group starting near you.* www.ActiveParenting.com

Communication Blocks Activity

We all use communication blocks at one time or another. Or, as one parent put it, "My skill is such that I can use three or four of these blocks at one time!" To catch ourselves before we block communication, it helps to know what our individual pitfalls are.

Think about the communication blocks you tend to use most often. Write them under "block" below. Then indicate the situations that usually bring them out, and what you see as your intention for using each block.

Situation	Block	Intention
Example: *Son didn't get the part in the school play.*	*Distracting*	*To make him feel better so I'd feel better.*

Active Listening Activity

Ramon: I don't believe it!

Sandra: You don't believe what?

Ramon: Mrs. Hickman. I was sitting there minding my own business while Caitlyn and Mark were passing notes back and forth and because I was between them they kept giving them to me to pass and then Mrs. Hickman turns around and sees me passing this note to Caitlyn… only it wasn't from me, it was from Mark. But Mrs. Hickman thought it was from me and gave me extra homework because I "apparently have so much time on my hands that I don't know what to do." It isn't fair!

Sandra: You sure sound angry.

Ramon: Yes! Wouldn't you?! I mean it wasn't even my note!

Sandra: And yet you're the one who got in trouble. I can see why you'd be upset.

Ramon: And then, Caitlynand Mark didn't say a word. They just sat there and giggled.

Sandra: You must have been furious about that.

Ramon: Yeah! They started it, and then let me take all the blame!

Sandra: And of course all Mrs. Hickman saw was you passing the note.

I guess you were a little embarrassed too, when Mrs. Hickman disciplined you in front of the whole class.

Ramon: Yeah. But the other kids saw what was going on, so it wasn't that bad. But now I have all this homework to do. It's not fair. I'm not going to do it.

Sandra: That's one thing you could do. What would happen if you don't do it?

Ramon: I guess Mrs. Hickman'd give me an "F" to average in with my grades.

Sandra: Ouch! That could really hurt, especially after all the hard work you've put in this year. What else could you do?

Ramon: I could tell her what really happened?

Sandra: Yes, you could. What do you think would happen then?

Ramon: Well...the other kids would probably call me a tattletale, and Mrs. Hickman would just tell me I had no business passing notes, anyway... that I should have ignored them.

Sandra: What do you think about that?

Ramon: I guess it was pretty dumb. I mean I guess I knew that she doesn't allow passing notes and all, but Mom, I didn't want the other kids to think I'm not cool.

Sandra: I see. You were afraid they wouldn't like you if you followed Mrs. Hickman's rules about no passing notes. So you let them get you in trouble because you want them to like you.

Ramon: Yeah. Pretty dumb, wasn't it?

Sandra: Well...let's put it this way: It's only dumb if you keep doing it. It may be a mistake that you can learn something from.

• • • • • • •

Sandra: Oh, Ramon. I've been meaning to ask—How did that passing notes problem work out? Did you do the extra homework?

Ramon: Yeah. I didn't think an "F" would be too great.

Sandra: And how about Mark and Caitlyn? Are they still trying to get you to pass notes in class?

Ramon: No way! I told them I didn't like what they did, and that the next time I was just going to just ignore them.

Sandra: Attaboy. I like the way you stood up for yourself. It's smart to not let people take advantage of you.

Responding to Feelings Video Practice

Scene	Child's Feeling	Parent's Response
Jenny and Li		
Matthew and Sherry		
Ben and Katy		
Alina and Carlos		
Angela and Sherry		
Ramon and Sandra		
Austin and Tim		

This worksheet refers to the 3-week Active Parenting Now in 3 *discussion program. If you are using this Parent's Guide independently and are interested in participating in a discussion group, check out the Parent tab at our website for a group starting near you.* www.ActiveParenting.com

Active Communication Evaluation

After you've had a chance to practice your active communication skills with one of your children this week, fill out the following evaluation so that you can be sure to learn from the experience.

What was the situation or problem that you talked to your child about?_____

_____

_____

How did you approach your child? _____

_____

_____

List examples of the five steps of active communication you were able to use:

1. Listen actively _____

_____

2. Listen for feelings _____

_____

3. Connect feelings to content _____

_____

4. Look for alternatives and evaluate consequences _____

_____

5. Follow up _____

_____

How did your child respond to your efforts? _____

_____

What did you like about how you handled the process?_____

_____

What would you do differently next time? _____

_____

Family Enrichment Activity

Taking Time for Fun

Remember when . . .

Remember something fun you enjoyed doing as a child with one of your parents. Close your eyes for a moment and visualize the pleasant experience.

What was the fun activity you and your parent shared? _____

_____

How did you feel about your parent at that moment? _____

_____

How did you feel about yourself? _____

_____

Have a family meeting to decide how you will take time for fun within the next week. Record what you decide. _____

_____

_____

Progress Chart

As you take time for fun with each of your children, record the experience below:

Child's name _____ What did you do? _____

_____

How did it go? _____

_____

Child's name _____ What did you do? _____

_____

How did it go? _____

_____

Child's name _____ What did you do? _____

_____

How did it go? _____

_____

Polite Requests, "I" Messages, and Firm Directions

1. Pretend that your child has just talked to you disrespectfully. Please write an example of a polite request that you could give your child:

   _____

   _____

2. Let's assume that your child continues to speak disprespectfully to you. Construct an "I" message that you could give your child:

   I have a problem with _____

   I feel _____

   because _____

   I would like (Will you please) _____

3. Let's assume that the "I" message was not effective. Construct a firm direction for your child:

   _____

Home Example

Write down a problem from your own family in which you own the problem. _____

_____

Now write an "I" message that you can use at home this week to solve the problem: _____

_____

When _____

I feel _____

because _____

I would like (Will you please) _____

Evaluation

How did your child respond to your "I" message? _____

_____

What did you like about the way you delivered the "I" message? _____

_____

How would you do it differently next time? _____

_____

Logical Consequences Video Practice

Scene	Guideline Violated	Possible Logical Consequences
1. Sherry *Matthew not getting up*		
2. Tim *Ben fighting*		
3. Sandra *Alina's music too loud*		
4. Sherry *Angela not eating her peas*		

This worksheet refers to the 3-week Active Parenting Now in 3 *discussion program. If you are using this Parent's Guide independently and are interested in participating in a discussion group, check out the Parent tab at our website for a group starting near you.* www.ActiveParenting.com

Using Logical Consequences

Think of a problem you would like to solve using a logical consequence. (You may choose the same problem for which you constructed an "I" message on page 112 as a back-up in case the "I" message is not effective.)

Write in the space below one way that you might present the choices and consequences to your child during the discussion of the problem. _____

_____

_____

Meet with your child to discuss the problem, and use this logical consequence or one that you develop with the child.

Evaluation

What was your child's response to the discussion? _____

_____

_____

What was his response to the logical consequence? (Did he test you to see if you would follow through?) _____

_____

If the consequence isn't working, do you think you need to stick with it longer or change the consequence to something else? _____

_____

If the consequence isn't working, have you violated any of the guidelines for setting up logical consequences? (Check page 90.) _____

What do you like about the way you handled the use of logical consequences? _____

_____

What will you do differently next time? _____

_____

Family Meeting: Problem-Prevention Talk

Before having your talk...

What topic will you discuss?

_____

_____

What are some specific concerns or risks that you want to share your thoughts and feelings about?

_____

_____

_____

_____

After your talk...

What guidelines did your family decide upon?

_____

_____

_____

_____

_____

What logical consequences or incentives, if any, did you include?

_____

_____

_____

_____

What went well during the meeting?

_____

_____

_____

What will you do differently next time?

_____

_____

How will you follow-up on the guidelines?

_____

_____

Family Enrichment Activity

Positive "I" Messages

Plan a positive "I" message, and then give it to one of your children this week.

I would like _____

I feel _____

Because _____

How about if I _____

Afterwards...

What did you like about how it went? _____

_____

_____

_____

_____

What will you do differently next time? _____

_____

_____

_____

_____

_____

Family Meeting: Problem-Prevention Talk

Before having your talk...

What topic will you discuss?

_____

_____

What are some specific concerns or risks that you want to share your thoughts and feelings about?

_____

_____

_____

_____

After your talk...

What guidelines did your family decide upon?

_____

_____

_____

_____

_____

What logical consequences or incentives, if any, did you include?

_____

_____

_____

What went well during the meeting?

_____

_____

What will you do differently next time?

_____

_____

How will you follow-up on the guidelines?

_____

_____

Stimulating Independence

Think of things that you are now doing for your children that they could be doing for themselves. For example, making their beds, picking up their clothes, cleaning up after them. Make a list below:

1. _____

2. _____

3. _____

4. _____

5. _____

6. _____

7. _____

8. _____

Now, choose one of these to let each child do for him- or herself this week. Be sure to be encouraging as you turn this over to each child, and practice our encouragement skills as each child progresses.

Afterwards . . .

What did you like about how it went? _____

_____

_____

_____

What can you do to improve things next time?_____

_____

_____

_____

Building on Strengths Activity: The BANK Method

Use the four steps of the BANK Method to encourage your child's progress in learning a skill or value. What is the goal that you would like to set for your child?

_____

Baby steps.

Write down five baby steps that your child will need to complete on the way to achieving this goal:

1. _____
2. _____
3. _____
4. _____
5. _____

Acknowledge what your child already does well. Write down three steps that your child has already mastered or strengths that will help your child achieve the goal:

1. _____
2. _____
3. _____

Next, talk with your child about the goal and acknowledge these strengths in the conversation. How did the talk go?

_____

Did you get your child's agreement to work on the goal together? If not, how will you approach your child differently next time? _____

_____

If your child agreed to work on the goal, fill in the final two steps after working together:

Nudge your child to take the next step. How did you encourage your child to take the next step? How did it go and what might you do to improve this next time? _____

_____

Keep encouraging improvement and persistence (especially after backsliding) until the goal is met. What words or actions did you find that were encouraging to your child? _____

_____

Showing Confidence

Find ways to encourage your child by showing confidence in one or more of the four ways detailed on pages 156 and 157. Then complete the questions for for the method(s) you chose.

1. What **responsibility** did you give your child? _____

_____

How did he or she handle it? _____

_____

How can you improve the situation? _____

_____

2. What did you **ask your child's advice** about? _____

_____

How did he or she respond? _____

_____

3. When did you **avoid the temptation to take over** for your child? _____

_____

How did you encourage your child to stick with it? _____

_____

How did he or she respond? _____

_____

4. When did you **show that you expected success or positive behavior**? _____

_____

How did he or she respond? _____

_____

What did you do to follow up? _____

_____

Valuing the Child

Find ways to show that you value your child for what she is, using one or more of the methods detailed on pages 160 and 161. Then complete the questions for for the method(s) you chose.

1. How did you **separate worth from accomplishments?** _____
   _____

   How did he or she respond? _____
   _____

   What would you do the same or different next time? _____
   _____

2. How did you **separate worth from mishbehavior?** _____
   _____

   How did he or she respond? _____
   _____

   What would you do the same or different next time? _____
   _____

3. How did you show that you **appreciate your child's uniqueness?** _____
   _____

   How did he or she respond? _____
   _____

   What would you do the same or different next time? _____
   _____

4. What special **words and actions** did you use to let your child know that you value him just for himself—unconditionally? _____
   _____

   How did he or she respond? _____
   _____

   What would you do the same or different next time? _____
   _____

Family Enrichment Activity

Letter of Encouragement

Remember when . . .

Recall a time when one of your parents said or did something that you found encouraging when you were a child. Take a moment to visualize the experience and to rekindle the positive feeling it provided.

What did your parent do or say? _____

_____

How did you feel? _____

_____

Now, try to find a letter or note that you found encouraging . . . from your parents or someone else.

What encouraged you about it? _____

_____

Use this space to write a rough draft of a letter of encouragement to each of your children. Then copy the letter onto stationery or other paper before placing it where your child will find it—or mailing it!

_____

_____

_____

_____

_____

_____

_____

_____

_____

_____

_____

_____

Family Meeting: Emphasizing the Family Unity

"In Our Family..."

Find a time to talk with your children about your family's history. You might include stories of how you came to this country or area, anecdotes about colorful family members, any special achievements and ways that you might honor their memories. Afterwards, answer these questions:

What special stories did you share? _____

_____

_____

_____

_____

_____

_____

How did your children respond? _____

_____

_____

_____

Did you record the experience by video or other means? _____

_____

_____

_____

What will you do to improve the experience next time? _____

_____

_____

_____

Goals for Active Parenting

List three things that you have learned from this guide:

1. _____
   _____

2. _____
   _____

3. _____
   _____

Do you feel that you've grown as a parent as a result of this guide? If so, how?

_____

_____

_____

_____

In what ways do you think the things you've learned have helped:

you? _____

_____

_____

your child or children? _____

_____

_____

your family? _____

_____

_____

10 Roles Parents Can Play in Preventing Problems with Drugs, Sexuality, and Violence

The Office of Substance Abuse Prevention (OSAP) suggests these 10 roles that parents can play in the prevention of drug use.

1. **Parents as role models.**
    Be a positive role model. Children learn best by example.

2. **Parents as educators and information resources.**
    Be informed about drugs, sexuality, and violence and talk with your child.

3. **Parents as policy makers and rule setters.**
    Make rules and enforce them. For example, "No use of illegal drugs by anyone in the family, and no use of alcohol or nicotine by anyone under the legal age."

4. **Parents as stimulators.**
    Encourage your child to take part in hobbies, school activities and sports. Get involved; plan fun family activities.

5. **Parents as consultants and educators on peer pressure.**
    "Just say no" is easier said than done. Teach your child to resist peer pressure without feeling foolish.

6. **Parents as monitors and supervisors.**
    Set and enforce curfews; know where your children are.

7. **Parents as collaborators with other parents.**
    Join with other parents to gain support and new ideas. There's strength in numbers.

8. **Parents as identifiers and confronters.**
    Know how to identify drug use and other problems and confront your child when necessary.

9. **Parents as managers of children's health.**
    Don't delay—seek medical help if you suspect your child is engaged in unhealthy behavior. Trust your instincts!

10. **Parents as managers of their own feelings.**
    Don't blow up; don't give up. You're not guilty.

This list is available as a large, color poster.
Contact Active Parenting Publishers for information.

NOTES

NOTES

NOTES

NOTES

It Doesn't Have to End!

If you found this course helpful, you'll also appreciate the many other resources offered by Active Parenting Publishers. Call for a catalog or visit our web site.

E-newsletter for Parents

Get parenting information from Dr. Popkin, tips about our latest products and more from the free Parents' E-newsletter! To sign up, just go to **www.ActiveParenting.com** and click on the "FREE" button.

Active Parenting Parents' Forum

Discuss experiences, ask questions, and share ideas in our special forum for parents! Just log on to our website at **www.ActiveParenting.com** and click on the "Parents" button.

Other Active Parenting Workshops

Additional workshops include: *1, 2, 3, 4, Parents!* (for parents of young children); *Active Parenting of Teens; Families in Action* (for parents and teens together or teen-only groups); *Windows: Healing and Helping through Loss; Parents on Board* (for promoting academic success in your children); and *Cooperative Parenting and Divorce* (for divorcing parents). Programs are also available in Spanish. Check our web site or ask your workshop leader if any of these courses are available in your area. If not, call our toll-free number and ask for a catalog to share with your local school, community center, or religious group.

Active Parenting Online Groups

Need a refresher course? Try the Active Parenting class online! These workshops "meet" over the Internet, where you can participate in live chats with other parents and a certified Active Parenting Online Leader. Go through the online course materials and watch the entertaining video vignettes (provided on CD ROM) at any time convenient to you during each week's session. For more information and to register, log on to our web site at www.ActiveParenting.com/Parents.

Active Parenting Catalog

Our catalog is filled with carefully selected books, videos and other resources that will help you be an active parent to your children as they grow. Contact us for a copy of the catalog.

Need More Active Parenting Now Parent's Guides?

Additional Parent's Guide are available at quantity discounts. It is also available in audio book format. Call for the latest pricing, or use our convenient online catalog at www.ActiveParenting.com.

For more information on these and other opportunities available from
Active Parenting Publishers, contact us!

(800) 825-0060 • fax (770) 429-0334
www.ActiveParenting.com

New from Active Parenting

Continue your Active Parenting experience or share it with another parent—or grand-parent! These products are a good refresher and make excellent gifts as well.

Active Parenting Online Groups

Experience an Active Parenting class online! These workshops "meet" over the Internet, where you can participate in live chats with other parents and a certified Active Parenting Online Leader. Go through the online course materials and watch the entertaining video vignettes (provided on CD ROM) at any time convenient to you during each week's session. For more information and to register, log on to our web site at **www.ActiveParenting.com/Parents**.

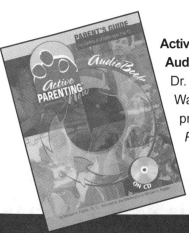

Active Parenting Now AudioBook

Dr. Michael Popkin and Joe Washington have teamed up to provide you with this unabridged, six-chapter *Active Parenting Now Parent's Guide* on CD. Whenever you need a refresher, listen to the CDs at home, in the car, while exercising...anytime! 296 minutes on 4 CDs.

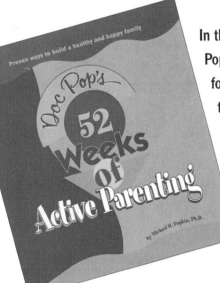